HIDDEN MICKEYS

A Field Guide to

Walt Disney World®'s

Best Kept Secrets

2nd edition

Steven M. Barrett

HIDDEN MICKEYS

A Field Guide to Walt Disney World®'s
Best Kept Secrets
2nd edition

Published by
The Intrepid Traveler
P.O. Box 531
Branford, CT 06405
http://www.intrepidtraveler.com

Copyright ©2005 by Steven M. Barrett
Second Edition
Printed in Canada
Cover design by Foster & Foster
Interior Design by Starving Artist Design Studio
Maps designed by Evora Taylor
Library of Congress Card Number: 2004113896
ISBN-13: 978-1-887140-56-0
ISBN-10: 1-887140-56-5

10 9 8 7 6 5 4 3 2 1

Trademarks, Etc. • • • • • • • • • • • • •

About the Author . . . .

Author Steven M. Barrett, paid his first visit to Disney World in the late 1980s, after attending a medical conference in Orlando. He immediately fell under its spell, visiting it twice yearly with family and friends for the next several years, offering touring advice to the less initiated, and reading almost everything written about the WDW theme parks. When a job in his field of emergency medicine opened up not far from WDW in 1998, Barrett, a Texas native, Air Force veteran, and former Oklahoma City medical professor, relocated to the Orlando area from Houston, Texas. He began visiting the WDW parks every chance he got to enjoy the attractions, sample the restaurants, and escort visiting friends and relatives. Eventually, feedback from family and friends made him realize he had better advice on touring the parks than they could get anywhere else. So he wrote the guidebook, *The Hassle-Free Walt Disney World® Vacation*, which includes customized touring plans for adults and teens, families with younger children, and seniors, along with lots of insider tips gleaned from his almost weekly visits to Disney World. His interest in Hidden Mickeys led him to take pen in hand once again. This book is the result. Enjoy!

Dedication •

I dedicate this book to my wife Vickie and
son Steven, who willingly accompanied me
on countless research visits to Disney World
and added invaluable insight to this book.

Read This First! . . . .

My guess is that you have visited Disney World before, perhaps many times. But if I've guessed wrong, and this is your first visit, then this note is for you.

Searching for Hidden Mickeys is lots of fun. But it's not a substitute for letting the magic of Disney sweep over you as you experience Walt Disney World (WDW) for first time. For one thing, the scavenger hunts I present in this book do not include all the attractions in WDW. That's because some of them don't have Hidden Mickeys! For another, this book omits many things the first-time visitor should know and do to make that first trip to Disney World as magical as possible.

So for first-time visitors (and repeat visitors looking for a way to experience the attractions with less hassle), I recommend my guide, *The Hassle-Free Walt Disney World® Vacation*. It contains up-to-date, customized touring plans for adults and teens, families with young children, and seniors, along with descriptions of all the WDW attractions, tips for planning your vacation, WDW restaurant ratings, and coverage of the WDW Resort hotels. You'll find it in bookstores or on the Web at TheOtherOrlando.com.

That doesn't mean you can't search for Hidden Mickeys, too. Just follow the suggestions in Chapter One of this book for "Finding Hidden Mickeys Without Scavenger Hunting."

Table of Contents • • • • • • • • • • • • •

Maps

True to their name, Hidden Mickeys are elusive. New ones appear from time to time and some old ones disappear (see page 14). When that happens — and it will — we will let you know on Steve's web site:

www.HiddenMickeysGuide.com

So if you can't find a Mickey — or if you're looking for just a few more — be sure to check it out.

CHAPTER 1

Hidden Mickey Mania

Have you ever marveled at a "Hidden Mickey?" People in the know often shout with glee when they recognize one. Some folks are so involved with discovering them that Hidden Mickeys can be visualized where none actually exist. These outbreaks of Hidden Mickey mania are confusing to the unenlightened. So let's get enlightened!

Here's the definition of an official Hidden Mickey: a partial or complete image of Mickey Mouse that has been hidden by Disney's Imagineers and artists in the designs of Disney attractions, hotels, restaurants, and other areas. These images are designed to blend into their surroundings. Sharp-eyed visitors have the fun of finding them.

The practice probably started as an inside joke among the Imagineers (the designers and builders of Disney attractions). According to Disney guru, Jim Hill (www.jimhillmedia.com), Hidden Mickeys originated in the late 1970s or early 1980s, when Disney management wanted to restrict Disney characters like Mickey and Minnie to the Magic Kingdom. The Imagineers designing Epcot couldn't resist slipping Mickeys into the new park, and thus "Hidden Mickeys" were born. Guests and "cast members" (Disney employees) started spotting them and the concept took on a life of its own. Today, Hidden Mickeys are anticipated in any new construction at Walt Disney World, and Hidden Mickey fans can't wait to find them.

Hidden Mickeys come in all sizes and many forms. The most common is an outline of Mickey's head formed by three intersecting circles, one for Mickey's round head and two for his round ears. Among Hidden Mickey fans, this image has been known as the "classic" Hidden Mickey, a term I will adopt in this book. Other Hidden Mickeys include a side or oblique (usually three-

9

quarter) profile of Mickey's face and head, a side profile of his entire body, a full-length silhouette of his body seen from the front, a detailed picture of his face or body, or a three-dimensional Mickey Mouse. Sometimes just his gloves, handprints, shoes or ears appear. Even his name or initials in unusual places may qualify as a Hidden Mickey.

And it's not just Mickeys that are hidden. The term "Hidden Mickey" also applies to hidden images of other popular characters. There are Hidden Minnies, Hidden Donald Ducks, Hidden Goofys, and other Hidden characters in Disney World, and I include many of them in this book.

The sport of finding Hidden Mickeys is catching on and adds even more interest to an already fun-filled Walt Disney World vacation. This book is your "field guide" to almost 500 Hidden Mickeys in WDW. To add to the fun, instead of just describing them, I've organized them into six scavenger hunts, one for each of the major theme parks, one for the Walt Disney World Resort hotels, and one for all the rest of WDW: the water parks, Downtown Disney, WDW Speedway, and beyond. The hunts are designed for maximum efficiency so that you can spend your time looking for Mickeys rather than cooling your heels in lines. Follow the Clues and you will find the best Hidden Mickeys WDW has to offer. If you have trouble spotting a particular Hidden Mickey (some are extraordinarily well camouflaged!) you can turn to the Hints at the end of each scavenger hunt for a fuller description.

Scavenger Hunting for Hidden Mickeys

To have the most fun and find the most Mickeys, follow these tips:

★ **Arrive early** for the theme park hunts, say 30 minutes before the official opening time. Pick up a Guidemap and plot your course. Then look for Hidden Mickeys in the waiting area while you wait for the rope to drop. You'll find the clues for those areas by checking the *Index to Mickey's Hiding Places* in the back of this book. Look under "Entrance areas." If you arrive later in the day, you may want to pick up a FASTPASS for the first attraction and then skip down a few clues to beat the crowds.

★ "Clues" and "Hints"

Clues under each attraction will guide you to the Hidden Mickey(s). If you have trouble spotting them, you can turn to the Hints at the end of the hunt for a fuller description. The Clues and Hints are numbered consecutively, that is, Hint 1 goes with Clue 1; so it's easy to find the right Hint if you need it. In some cases, *Test Track* in Epcot is a notable example, you may have to ride the attraction more than once to find all the Hidden Mickeys.

★ Scoring

All Hidden Mickeys are fun to find, but all Hidden Mickeys aren't the same. Some are easier to find than others. I assign point values to Hidden Mickeys, identifying them as easy to spot (a value of 1 point) to difficult to find the first time (5 points). I also consider the complexity and uniqueness of the image: the more complex or unique the Hidden Mickey, the higher the point value. For example, the easy-to-spot Hidden Mickeys in Mickey's Toontown Fair in Magic Kingdom are one-point Mickeys. The brilliantly camouflaged Mickey hiding in the *Body Wars* mural in Epcot is a five-pointer.

★ Playing the game

You can hunt solo or with others; competitively or just for fun. There's room to tally your score in the guide. Families with young children may want to focus on one- and two-point Mickeys that the little ones will have no trouble spotting. (Of course, little ones tend to be sharp-eyed; so they may spot familiar shapes before you do in some of the more complex patterns.) Or you may want to split your party into teams and see who can rack up the most points (in which case, you'll probably want to have a guide for each team).

Of course, you don't have to play the game at all. You can simply look for Hidden Mickeys in attractions as you come to them (see "Finding Hidden Mickey's Without Scavenger Hunting," below).

★ Following the clues

The hunts often call for crisscrossing the parks. This may seem illogical at first, but trust me, it will keep you ahead of the crowds. Besides, it adds to the fun of the hunt and, if you're playing competitively, keeps everyone on their toes.

★ Waiting in line

Don't waste time in lines. If the wait is longer than 15 minutes, get a FASTPASS (if available and you're eligible), move on to the next attraction, and come back at your FASTPASS time. *Exception:* In some attractions, the Hidden Mickey(s) can only be seen from the queue line, and not the FASTPASS line. (I've not suggested FASTPASS in the Clues section when that is the case.) The lines at these attractions should not be too long if you start your scavenger hunt when the park opens and follow the hunt clues as given. If you do encounter long lines, come back later during a parade or in the hour before the park closes. Alternatively, use the singles line if available.

★ Playing fair

Be considerate of other guests. Many Hidden Mickeys are in restaurants and shops. Ask a cast member's permission before searching inside sit-down restaurants, and avoid the busy mealtime hours unless you are one of the diners. Tell the cast members and other guests who see you looking around what you're up to, so they can share in the fun.

Finding Hidden Mickeys Without Scavenger Hunting

If scavenger hunts don't appeal to you, you don't have to use them. You can find Hidden Mickeys in the specific rides and other attractions you visit by using the *Index to Mickey's Hiding Places* in the back of this book. For easy lookup, attractions in Magic Kingdom and Disney's Animal Kingdom are also listed under their appropriate "lands" (for example, Fantasyland in Magic Kingdom and Asia in Animal Kingdom). In Epcot, attractions are listed alphabetically and by Pavilion. To find Hidden Mickeys in the attraction, restaurant, hotel or shop you are visiting, turn to the Index, locate the appropriate page, and follow the Clue(s) to find the Hidden Mickey(s).

Caution: You won't find every WDW attraction, restaurant, hotel or shop in the Index. Only those with confirmed Hidden Mickeys are included in this guide.

Hidden Mickeys, "Gray Zone" Mickeys, Wishful Thinking

For every "official" or well-accepted Hidden Mickey, there are two or more "gray zone" Hidden Mickeys. These Mickeys may not be well hidden or may have distorted proportions—ears that aren't round or are too close together or too far apart, for example. Yet they are often accepted as Hidden Mickeys by observers. Examples include the various classic (three-circle) Hidden Mickey-shaped locks you'll see in a number of attractions, such as the jail cell lock in *Pirates of the Caribbean* in Magic Kingdom. I include some of these gray-zone Mickeys in this book, although some enthusiasts may argue the merits of specific choices.

Other Hidden Mickeys are sentimental favorites with Disney fans, even though they may actually represent "wishful thinking." For example, the "three-gears classic Mickey" at *Big Thunder Mountain Railroad* in Magic Kingdom is not proportioned quite right and so is a bit of a stretch. But many guests and even cast members call the gears a Hidden Mickey, and I'll admit, I rather like it myself. So you will find it in the *Magic Kingdom Scavenger Hunt* in Chapter 2, Clue 3).

The classic (three-circle) Mickeys are the most controversial, for good reason. Much debate surrounds the gathering of circular forms throughout Walt Disney World. The large classic Hidden Mickey outlined in the cement at the rear of Africa in Disney's Animal Kingdom (Clue 48 in the *Animal Kingdom Scavenger Hunt*), is obviously the work of a clever artist. But classic (i.e., three-circle) configurations occur spontaneously in art and nature, as in collections of grapes, tomatoes, pumpkins, bubbles, oranges, cannonballs, and the like. Unlike the Hidden Mickey in Africa, it may be difficult to attribute a specific "classic Mickey" configuration to a deliberate Imagineer design.

So which groupings of three qualify as Hidden Mickeys? Unfortunately, no master list of actual or "Imagineer-approved" Hidden Mickeys exists. Walt Disney World attempts to keep an "official" Hidden Mickey list (accessible from its websites) but even it is incomplete! The most exhaustive compilation resides at the HiddenMickeys.org website, a resource worthy of a visit by any Hidden Mickey enthusiast. However, a number of the reported sightings there are stretches of the imagination, or "wishful thinking," as credible verification is often hard to come by. (My neighbor, Lew Brooks, calls them "two-beer" Mickeys.)

Purists demand that a true classic Hidden Mickey have proper proportions. The round head must be larger than the ear circles, so that three equal circles in the proper alignment would not qualify as a Hidden Mickey. My own criteria are a bit looser. If three circles approximate the correct proportions and alignment, especially if they stand apart from the pack or if they've been identified by other observers, I include them in this book as Hidden Mickeys.

Hidden Mickeys vs. Decorative Mickeys

Some Mickeys are truly hidden, not visible to the tourist. They may be located behind the scenes, accessible only to cast members. You won't find them in this field guide for obvious reasons. Other Mickeys are decorative; they were placed in plain sight to enhance the décor. For example, in a restaurant, I consider a pat of butter shaped like Mickey Mouse to be a decorative (aka décor) Mickey. Disney World is loaded with decorative Mickeys. You'll find images of Mickey Mouse on items ranging from manhole covers, to laundry room soap dispensers, to toilet paper

 wrappers and shower curtains in the hotels. I do not include these ubiquitous and sometimes changing images in this book unless they are unique or hard to spot.

Hidden Mickeys can change or be accidentally removed over time, by the process of nature or by the continual cleaning and refurbishing that goes on at Disney World. For example, at Disney-MGM Studios, cables coiled to form a classic Mickey in the pre-show viewing area of *Rock 'n' Roller Coaster Starring Aerosmith* recently disappeared. Cast members themselves sometimes create or remove Hidden Mickeys.

My Selection Process

I trust you've concluded by now that Hidden Mickey Science is an evolving specialty. Which raises the question, how did I choose the almost 500 Hidden Mickeys in the scavenger hunts in this guide? I compiled my list of Hidden Mickeys from all resources to which I had access, my own sightings, friends, family, cast members, websites, and books. (Cast members in each specific area usually — but not always! — know where some Hidden Mickeys are located.) Then I did my own hunts, and I took along friends or family to verify my sightings. I have included only Hidden Mickeys I could verify.

Furthermore, some Hidden Mickeys are visible only intermittently or only from certain vantage points in ride vehicles. I don't generally include these Mickeys, unless I feel that adequate descriptions will allow anyone to find them. So the scavenger hunts include only those images I believe to be recognizable as Hidden Mickeys and visible to the general touring guest. It is likely, though, that one or more of the Hidden Mickeys described in this book will disappear over time.

I'll try to let you know when I discover that a Hidden Mickey has disappeared for good by posting the information on my website:

www.HiddenMickeysGuide.com

If you find one missing before I do, email me care of my publisher's website to let me know:

sbarrett@TheOtherOrlando.com

I have enjoyed finding each and every Hidden Mickey in this book. I'm certain I'll find more as time goes by, and I hope you can spot new Hidden Mickeys during your visit.

So put on some comfortable walking shoes and experience Walt Disney World like you never have before!

Happy Hunting!

— Steve Barrett

CHAPTER 2

Magic Kingdom Scavenger Hunt

Clue 1: Examine the scrollwork of the roof of the Main Street Train Station.
2 points

While you are waiting for the park to open you may want to hunt for Hidden Mickeys on Main Street U.S.A. (See clues 85 to 88.)

Go to **Space Mountain**. Mickey isn't hiding there but you will find a Hidden Character along the exit from the ride.

Clue 2: Look for a shadow of Winnie the Pooh along the moving exit walkway.
4 points

(Don't get discouraged. This one is hard to spot. That's why it's worth 4 points!)

Note: There aren't any Hidden Mickeys on the ride itself. So you can skip the ride if roller coasters aren't your thing or you want to focus on your Hidden Mickey hunt. Just line up for the ride. Then when you reach the vehicle loading dock, ask a cast member to show you to the exit area. Tell them you're looking for Hidden Mickeys.

★ Cross the park to Frontierland and get a FASTPASS to ride *Splash Mountain* later. Then ride **Big Thunder Mountain Railroad**.

Clue 3: Look for a classic Hidden Mickey on the ground to your right near the end of the ride.
2 points

★ Return to **Splash Mountain** at your allotted FASTPASS time. Hop aboard and keep your eyes peeled for five Hidden Mickeys on the ride and two more after you exit.

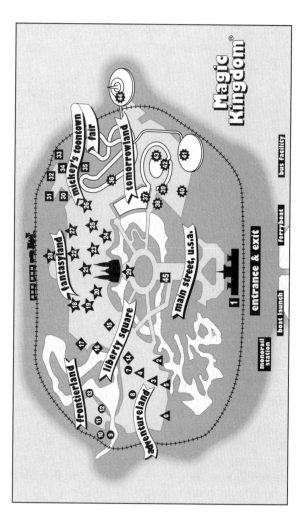

1 WDW Railroad, Entrance

adventureland

2 Swiss Family Treehouse

3 The Enchanted Tiki Room Under New Management

4 The Magic Carpets of Aladdin

5 Jungle Cruise

6 Pirates of the Caribbean

frontierland

7 Frontierland Shootin' Arcade

8 Country Bear Jamboree

9 Splash Mountain

10 WDW Railroad

11 Big Thunder Mountain Railroad

12 Raft to Tom Sawyer Island

13 Mike Fink Keelboats (currently closed)

liberty square

14 Character Show/Greeting Area

15 The Hall of Presidents

16 Liberty Square Riverboat

17 The Haunted Mansion

fantasyland

18 "it's a small world"

19 Peter Pan's Flight

20 Mickey's PhilharMagic

21 Cinderella's Golden Carrousel

22 Dumbo the Flying Elephant

23 Snow White's Scary Adventures

24 Fairytale Garden

25 The Many Adventures of Winnie the Pooh

26 Mad Tea Party

27 Fantasyland Character Festival

28 Ariel's Grotto

29 Castle Forecourt Stage

mickey's toontown fair

30 Minnie's Country House

31 Toontown Hall Of Fame

32 Mickey's Country House

33 WDW Railroad

34 Donald's Boat

35 The Barnstormer at Goofy's Wiseacre Farm

tomorrowland

36 Tomorrowland Indy Speedway

37 Stitch's Great Escape!

38 The Timekeeper

39 Buzz Lightyear's Space Ranger Spin

40 Galaxy Palace Theater

41 Walt Disney's Carousel of Progress

42 Tomorrowland Transit Authority

43 Astro Orbiter

44 Space Mountain

main street, u.s.a.

45 Guest Information Board

Clue 4: Soon after you start, search for barrels that form a classic Mickey.
3 points

Clue 5: Just past Brer Frog, find the fishing bobbers that form a Hidden Mickey.
3 points

Clue 6: In the room with jumping water, spot the hanging rope classic Mickey.
5 points

Clue 7: As your boat ascends toward the big drop, look toward the opening for a side profile of Mickey's face.
3 points

Clue 8: In the riverboat scene after the big drop, find the Hidden Mickey in the clouds.
4 points

Clue 9: Along the exit walkway, look for the birdhouse with an acorn classic Mickey.
3 points

Clue 10: After the ride, take another look at the mountain from the outside viewing area to spot that side profile (again).
3 points

★ Take a short break and grab some refreshment in Frontierland or Liberty Square, which has a good fruit stand. Afterward: Stop by the **Frontierland Shootin' Arcade**.

Clue 11: Find a classic Mickey in front of the target area.
1 point

★ Then turn right to the **Liberty Tree Tavern** and walk inside.

Clue 12: Explore the rear wall of the Tavern's waiting area to find a classic Hidden Mickey.
2 points

20

★ Cross the street.

Clue 13: Find the classic Hidden Mickeys on the stocks near the **Liberty Square Riverboat** entrance.
1 point

★ Head for **The Haunted Mansion**. (Get a FAST-PASS if the wait is too long.) Find three classic Mickeys while you enjoy the ride.

Clue 14: In the first room inside the entrance, look for some classic Mickeys in the border design around a portrait.
3 points

Clue 15: During the ride, find the Mickey on the ghostly banquet table.
2 points

Clue 16: Spot the pots across the ride tracks from the woman with the red, beating heart.
4 points

Clue 17: Look closely at the "grim reaper" by the opera singing lady.
5 points

Clue 18: Outside, as you exit, look down for a classic Mickey next to a gate.
3 points

★ Enter the **Columbia Harbour House Restaurant** and look for a classic Hidden Mickey. (Be considerate of the diners.)

Clue 19: Check the art on the downstairs walls.
2 points

★ Walk into Frontierland and take the first passage to your left into Adventureland. Ride the **Pirates of the Caribbean** and find three classic Hidden Mickeys.

Clue 20: Try to spot the classic Mickey shadow above the drunken pirate's cat.
4 points

Clue 21: Near the end of the ride, observe the lock on the jail cell door.
1 point

Clue 22: In the final scene, look for a classic Mickey shadow from a lamp.
3 points

★ Head for Tomorrowland. In the circle at the end of Main Street (near Cinderella Castle), examine the **statues of Walt Disney and Mickey Mouse**.

Clue 23: Check out the shadows around the base of the statues.
2 points

★ Now cross the bridge to Tomorrowland and go to the **Tomorrowland Indy Speedway.**

Clue 24: Look for a shadow on the pavement near the Speedway that's shaped like a classic Mickey.
3 points

Clue 25: Walk inside the Grandstand Viewing area (near the exit to the Indy ride) and up the stairs to find the Mickey ears on one of the billboards.
4 points

★ Enjoy an early lunch (11:00 a.m.) to avoid the crowds. Suggestions: the Plaza Restaurant off Main Street for sit-down or Cosmic Ray's Starlight Café in Tomorrowland for a sandwich.

★ After lunch, walk to **Mickey's Toontown Fair**. (Note: Some Hidden Mickey hunters might consider most of the Mickeys in this area décor Mickeys, rather than Hidden Mickeys. But they are such fun to pick out that I have included many of them in the hunt.)

Clue 26: Keep your eyes peeled as you walk through the street.
1 point

★ Go to **Minnie's Country House**.

Clue 27: Spot the Mickey on the outside chimney.
3 points

★ Now step inside Minnie's house.

Clue 28: Find yellow and blue classic Hidden Mickeys in Minnie's sewing room.
1 point for yellow, 1 point for blue

Clue 29: Observe the pots and pans in Minnie's kitchen to find another classic Mickey.
1 point

★ Stroll over to **Mickey's Country House**. Mickey's house and garden are loaded with classic Hidden Mickeys: Try to find 14 Mickeys plus a hidden Donald Duck.

Clue 30: You'll find four classic Mickeys on the way in.
1 point each

Clue 31: Look for two more just inside the front door.
1 point each

Clue 32: There's one in Mickey's bedroom.
1 point

Clue 33: Now find two classic Mickeys and a Donald in the game room.
1 point each

Clue 34: Explore Mickey's backyard (behind his house) and find at least three classic Mickeys.
1 point each

Clue 35: Check the walls and shelves of Mickey's garage for two Hidden Mickeys.
1 point each

★ Now check out the **Judge's Tent** to earn some possible bonus points.
1 bonus point for each HM you spot.

★ Go to **The Barnstormer at Goofy's Wiseacre Farm**. (You can skip the main ride if you want.)

Clue 36: Along the entrance queue, find the Hidden Mickey near the silo. Psst! It's a side profile.
2 points

★ Stroll toward **Cinderella Castle**.

Clue 37: Find the classic Mickey shadows along the curved walkway to the Castle.
2 points

★ Cross the main bridge to Tomorrowland and get a FASTPASS for *Buzz Lightyear's Space Ranger Spin*.

Clue 38: Spot the classic Mickey on the FASTPASS machine.
2 points

★ Go to the outside of **The Timekeeper** (open seasonally and on busy holidays).

Clue 39: Find the moon with classic Mickey craters.
1 point

Clue 40: Spot the asteroid shaped like a classic Mickey.
1 point

★ See **The Timekeeper** (if open).

Clue 41: In the scene when 9-Eye accidentally returns to modern Paris, spot the Mickey balloon.
3 points

★ Go to the **Carousel of Progress** (open seasonally and on busy holidays). Look for four Hidden Mickeys in the last scene:

Clue 42: Observe a painting on the rear wall.
4 points

Clue 43: Find a Mickey nutcracker.
1 point

Clue 44: Spot a Mickey Mouse doll.
1 point.

Clue 45: View an object with Mickey ears in the kitchen.
1 point

★ Go to **Buzz Lightyear's Space Ranger Spin** at your allotted FASTPASS time and be on the lookout for five Hidden Mickeys.

Clue 46: Inside the building on the right wall, find the planet with a continent shaped like the side profile of Mickey Mouse.
2 points

Clue 47: Look for this same planet further along the entrance queue to the left.
2 points

Clue 48: During the first part of the ride, spot a different side profile of Mickey. Look to the left of your vehicle in the room with batteries.
3 points

Clue 49: Watch for the planet with Mickey again in the space video room.
3 points

Clue 50: Just past the space video room, look straight ahead to spot that Mickey planet one more time.
2 points

★ Walk to the far side of **Astro Orbiter** and search carefully for a small classic Mickey indented in the cement nearby.

Clue 51: Check the side facing *Space Mountain*.
5 points

★ Go to the **Liberty Square Riverboat** (it sometimes closes at 5:00 p.m. or at dusk). If the wait is 10 minutes or more, grab a snack from a vendor in Liberty Square or Frontierland and refresh yourself while you wait to ride the boat.

Clue 52: On the boat, look for a classic Mickey rock formation at the right end of the bridge in Frontierland.
4 points

★ Head for **Fantasyland**. Check out the waiting times for *The Many Adventures of Winnie the Pooh*, *Snow White's Scary Adventures*, and *Peter Pan's Flight*. Get a FASTPASS for *Winnie the Pooh* (if available), then ride the other two if the waits are 20 minutes or less. Search for Hidden Mickeys as you go.

If the waits are long, return to enjoy these rides during a parade or in the hour before park closing.

★ Try to find four Hidden Mickeys as you enjoy **Snow White's Scary Adventures**. Look for the first two in the mural in the loading area.

Clue 53: Find a red classic Mickey on the Dwarves' laundry.
3 points

Clue 54: Look for three gray stones that form another classic Mickey.
2 points

Clue 55: During the ride, look closely behind the Wicked Queen to find a classic Mickey.
1 point

Clue 56: Then keep your eyes peeled for Mickey Mouse dressed as a Dwarf.
4 points

★ Go to **Peter Pan's Flight**.

Clue 57: Just before you get to the entrance queue turnstile, look closely at the bark of the trees facing the loading area to find a classic Hidden Mickey.
3 points

Clue 58: Search for alphabet blocks in the ride that spell two famous names.
4 points

★ Ride **The Many Adventures of Winnie the Pooh** (or return during your FASTPASS window) and look for three Hidden characters. Psst! Mr. Toad appears twice.

26

Clue 59: Examine the flower pot marker in Rabbit's Garden.
3 points

Clue 60: In Owl's house, find the picture of Mr. Toad and Owl.
3 points

Clue 61: Near the end of Owl's house, locate another picture of Mr. Toad with Winnie the Pooh.
3 points

★ See **Mickey's PhilharMagic** or get a FASTPASS to enjoy it later if the wait is too long.

Clue 62: In the first waiting area inside, squint at the wall mural.
3 points

Clue 63: Inside the main theatre, examine the border of the video screen.
2 points

★ Enter the **Pinocchio Village Haus Restaurant**.

Clue 64: Look for a tiny classic Mickey on the wall near the exit to the restrooms.
4 points

★ Walk to Cinderella Castle and ask a cast member for permission to stroll around **Cinderella's Royal Table Restaurant** to look for classic Hidden Mickeys. (Be considerate of the diners and staff.)

Clue 65: Check the ceiling.
2 points

★ Stroll over to **Fairytale Garden**.

Clue 66: Find a classic Mickey on a column.
3 points

Clue 67: Search for a Hidden Character on a wall.
4 points

★ Ride **"it's a small world"** and try to spot three classic Hidden Mickeys.

Clue 68: In the Africa room, look up at the vine with purple leaves.
2 points

Clue 69: In the South Pacific room, study the clown's hairdo.
2 points

Clue 70: On the right wall along the up-ramp exit, observe the flower patterns.
2 points

★ As you exit, head toward **Peter Pan's Flight**.

Clue 71: Gaze at the clouds forming the entrance sign.
3 points

Clue 72: Find grapes arranged like a classic Mickey.
2 points

★ Stop near **The Yankee Trader** shop.

Clue 73: Look down at hoofprints.
4 points

★ Head for Adventureland and pick up a FASTPASS for *Jungle Cruise*, if available. Then go and see **"The Enchanted Tiki Room Under New Management."**

Clue 74: Find classic Mickeys at the bottom of two bird perches, one in the left corner as you enter and the other in the right corner as you exit.
3 points each

★ Eat an early dinner either before or after riding *Jungle Cruise*. One choice: The Crystal Palace buffet. Disney characters visit your table there, but priority seating reservations are usually needed unless you're both early and lucky.

★ Ride **Jungle Cruise** during your FAST-PASS window and search for two Hidden Mickeys.

Clue 75: In the Cambodian Temple ruins, look for a classic Hidden Mickey near the treasure.
2 points

Clue 76: Coming out of the temple, look hard at the first undecorated column on the left for a chipped area of brick that forms part of a profile of Mickey's head and face. (This is a tough one!)
5 points

★ Cross the park to Tomorrowland and go to **Tomorrowland Transit Authority**. Find a Hidden Mickey as you ride.

Clue 77: In the last part of the ride, observe the accessories of the woman getting her hair done.
2 points

★ Walk by the **Merchant of Venus** shop.

Clue 78: Study the display windows.
2 points

★ Now scan the wall mural inside **Mickey's Star Traders Shop**.

Clue 79: Look for the train on the mural.
2 points

Clue 80: Find the Hidden Stitch.
3 points

Clue 81: Spot Mickey hats on a building.
2 points

Clue 82: Look up higher at the satellite dishes.
2 points

Clue 83: Scan the mural for the road formation.
3 points

Clue 84: Follow the mural around to another classic Mickey on a building.
1 point

★ Cross the nearest bridge to **Main Street** and search for four classic Mickeys as you stroll toward the park entrance.

Clue 85: Inside the Emporium store, study the merchandise stands.
2 points

Clue 86: Observe the overhead moving candy bins in the Main Street Confectionary near Town Square.
2 points

Clue 87: Closely examine the Caffe Italiano coffee cart (present seasonally) near Tony's Town Square Restaurant.
2 points

Clue 88: Look to the right of the entrance to Tony's Town Square Restaurant for the Goofy Pose-A-Matic classic Mickey.
1 point

★ End your scavenger hunt by riding the **WDW Railroad** around the park to search out one more Hidden Mickey.

Clue 89: Try to spot the reclining Mickey in the clouds as your train chugs through *Splash Mountain*.
4 points

Total Points for Magic Kingdom =

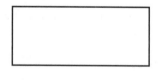

How'd you do?
Up to 92 points - Bronze
93 - 185 points - Silver
186 points and over - Gold
232 points - Perfect Score

(If you earned bonus points in the *Judge's Tent*, you may have done even better!)

**Caution:
Don't peek at this
section unless you
really want help!**

Main Street

- Train Station

Hint 1: The periphery of the Main Street Train Station roof, second level, has scrollwork that repeats a classic Mickey motif.

Tomorrowland

- Space Mountain

Hint 2: In the second scene to your right along the moving walkway at the ride exit, a shadow of Winnie the Pooh repeatedly moves right to left across a large hole in a rock.

Frontierland

- Big Thunder Mountain Railroad

Hint 3: At the end of the ride, just past the

dinosaur bones on the right side of the track, you'll see sets of gear wheels lying on the ground. The second set of gears resembles a classic Hidden Mickey. (The dimensions aren't quite classic, but this is a sentimental favorite.)

- Splash Mountain

Hint 4: Halfway up the second crankhill, on the right side, three barrels in the lower right corner of a stack of barrels form a classic Mickey.

Hint 5: Look for a picnic basket up on a small ledge. You'll spot it just past Brer Frog, who is sitting on an alligator and fishing with his toe. Near the basket are three red-and-white-striped fishing bobbers in the shape of a classic Hidden Mickey.

Hint 6: On the right side of your boat, in the room with jumping water, a classic rope Mickey is hanging halfway down from the ceiling. It's in the shadows behind a lantern and just past the turtle lying on a geyser.

Hint 7: The hole in the mountain at the top of the big drop is sculpted to form a side profile of Mickey's face. Mickey's nose juts out from the left side of the hole. (You can also see this one from the outside viewing area; see Hint 10).

Hint 8: Near the end of the ride, the upper outline of one of the white clouds on the right side of the riverboat scene is shaped like Mickey Mouse lying on his back, with his head to the right. (This Hidden Mickey is also visible from the *Walt Disney World Railroad* as it passes through *Splash Mountain*.)

Hint 9: A birdhouse with a rope ladder in the entrance queue (visible as you exit) has a classic Mickey acorn formation above a door and below blue roof slats. You'll find it just past the photo viewing area.

Hint 10: Walk in front of *Splash Mountain* after your ride. The hole in the mountain for the big drop forms a side profile of

Mickey's face. From the outside, Mickey's nose juts out from the right side of the hole.

- Frontierland Shootin' Arcade

Hint 11: In the front center of the target area is a group of cactus plants. One near the middle has three lobes forming a classic Hidden Mickey.

Liberty Square

- Liberty Tree Tavern Restaurant

Hint 12: Look for a spice rack to the right of the fireplace, on the rear wall of the waiting area. A small still-life painting on the spice rack includes three grapes that form a classic Mickey.

- Stocks near the Liberty Square Riverboat entrance

Hint 13: Padlocks on the stocks near the entrance are shaped like classic Hidden Mickeys.

- The Haunted Mansion

Hint 14: Just inside the entrance of the first room, you'll find some small classic Mickeys in the oval border design around the portrait of the dressed-up aging man above the fireplace.

Hint 15: A plate and two saucers on the ghostly banquet table are arranged to form a classic Mickey. They're usually at the bottom left corner of the table.

Hint 16: Directly across the track from the woman with the red, beating heart, three pots forming a classic Mickey are stuck on a vertical beam above and to the left of your "Doom Buggy."

Hint 17: To the right of the opera singing lady (her left) is a ghost resembling the grim reaper. He is holding up his left arm. Hanging from his left hand is a cloth with markings at the top that form a classic Hidden Mickey.

Hint 18: Outside, at the left end of the covered walk-way, a classic Mickey metal latch holds a wrought iron gate open. (Thanks to Paul Hoffman for this HM.)

- Columbia Harbour House Restaurant

Hint 19: In the downstairs table area, a wall across from the food-order counters is decorated with three small circular maps covered by a single piece of glass. (The central map is labeled Charles V.) The three circles form a classic Mickey.

Adventureland

- Pirates of the Caribbean

Hint 20: About halfway through the ride and past the red-haired lady, a cat behind an intoxicated pirate casts a classic Hidden Mickey moving shadow on the corner of the wall above and behind it.

Hint 21: Near the end of the ride, the lock on the jail cell door resembles a classic Mickey. Even though the dimensions aren't quite right, many folks, myself included, consider this a sentimental favorite Hidden Mickey.

Hint 22: In the final scene, the shadow from the bottom of the last flickering lamp on the wall to the left of the boat forms a small classic Mickey.

Walt and Mickey statues on Main Street

Hint 23: A small railing encircles the base of the statues and casts shadows on both the walkway around them and on the wall on which the railing sits. The dark part of the bottom of those shadows contains classic Mickeys.

Tomorrowland

- Near and in Tomorrowland Indy Speedway

Hint 24: A tall lamp post casts a classic Mickey shadow on the pavement. It's best seen during the late morning or early afternoon.

Hint 25: Visible from the Grandstand Viewing area, the third billboard back from the overhead exit walkway ("Indy Time Trials") sports a small pair of Mickey ears below the lower knee of the silhouette of a man flying through the air.

Mickey's Toontown Fair

Hint 26: On the streets, look for classic Hidden Mickeys on the upper edges of the merchandise carts.

- approaching and in Minnie's Country House

Hint 27: The front of the chimney outdoors includes three stones that form a classic Mickey. They are just left of where the roof and chimney meet.

Hint 28: In Minnie's sewing room, a large quilt on the wall has yellow classic Mickey heads on every other square and a blue classic Mickey in the center of the blue ribbon.

Hint 29: Over the stove in Minnie's kitchen, a frying pan and two pots form a classic Mickey head.

- approaching, in and around Mickey's Country House

Hint 30: As you head into the house, look for classic Mickeys:
- on the mailbox in front.
- on top of the front fence.
- above the front bay window.
- on the front door.

Hint 31: Just inside the front door of the house, observe more classic Mickeys on:
- the handle of an umbrella in the umbrella stand to the left.
- the mirror.

Hint 32: Look along the edge of the rug in Mickey's bedroom for more classic Mickeys.

Hint 33: In the game room, first check the shape of the checkers on the checkerboard. Then look closely at the ping-pong paddles: one is shaped like Mickey's head and the other like Donald's.

Hint 34: The design and contents of Mickey's back-yard change periodically, but here are a few classic Mickeys you are likely to see:
- the hedge and grass garden together form Mickey's head. The grass is the head and the hedge forms his ears.
- tomato Mickeys.
- pumpkin Mickeys.

Hint 35: In Mickey's garage, three hubcaps on the upper back wall form a classic Hidden Mickey, and you'll find Mickey ears on a shelf, sculpted out of hay.

- in the Judge's Tent

The interior arrangements of this attraction change frequently, so I don't know what Hidden Mickeys you may find when you visit. You can count on seeing a number of décor Mickeys if you decide to wait long enough to meet Mickey (and it will be a wait!). Just keep your eyes open. In the Main Mouse's room, ex-amine the walls closely for a classic Mickey in the centers of blue ribbons decorating the walls and give yourself an extra bonus point.

- The Barnstormer at Goofy's Wiseacre Farm

Hint 36: Along the entrance queue, a weather vane outside (above the silo on the right) has the shape of Mickey's side profile.

Walkway to Cinderella Castle

Hint 37: The circle patterns in the railings along the curved walkway approaching the entrance to the Castle cast classic Mickey shadows on the pavement. If the shadows aren't well formed when you pass, come by again later in the afternoon.

Tomorrowland

Hint 38: On the right side of the display at the top of the FASTPASS machines for *Buzz Lightyear's Space Ranger Spin* is a classic Mickey with red ears.

- The Timekeeper

Hint 39: On the outside wall, a picture advertising a Recreational Rocket has a moon with craters shaped like an upside down classic Mickey.

Hint 40: Also on the outside wall, a sign advertising a Space Collectibles Convention includes an asteroid shaped like a classic Mickey head.

Hint 41: In *The Timekeeper* movie, there is a very short scene in which 9-Eye accidentally returns to modern Paris (a rock band is playing on the right side of the screen). In that scene, a young girl on the screen behind Timekeeper is holding a balloon with Mickey's face on one side.

- Carousel of Progress (last scene)

Hint 42: An abstract Mickey Mouse as the Sorcerer's apprentice from *Fantasia* is in a painting on the dining room wall. To spot it, look immediately to the left rear of the scene as it rotates into view. The painting is on the dining room's right wall.

Hint 43: On the left side of the room, a nutcracker shaped like Mickey Mouse stands on the left side of the mantelpiece.

Hint 44: Under the Christmas tree is a box with a plush Mickey Mouse.

Hint 45: A pepper grinder on the kitchen counter has Mickey ears.

- Buzz Lightyear's Space Ranger Spin

Hint 46: Just inside the building, in the entrance queue, the second poster on the right wall is called "Planets of the Galactic

Alliance." In Sector One, the central continent on the planet "Pollost Prime" is shaped like a profile of Mickey Mouse's head in outline.

Hint 47: This same planet appears in the top left of a recessed wall further along the entrance queue, to the left of the large View Master.

Hint 48: You go through three different rooms during the first part of this ride. When you enter the room with lots of batteries, look to the left of the ride vehicle. You'll see a side profile of Mickey's head in the rear left under the words, "Initiate Battery Unload."

Hint 49: As the ride vehicle moves through the space video room, planet "Pollost Prime" with continent Mickey flies by on the right wall.

Hint 50: Just past the space video room, in the final battle scene on the ride, "Pollost Prime" shows up yet again on a wall straight ahead and to the upper left.

- Astro Orbiter

Hint 51: A small classic Mickey is indented in the cement close to a support beam near *Astro Orbiter* on the side toward *Space Mountain*, between Cool Ship and The Lunching Pad.

Liberty Square

- Liberty Square Riverboat

Hint 52: At the right end of the bridge from Frontierland (as you face it from the boat), three rocks form a classic Mickey. They're located between the last two vertical posts that support the handrail, about one foot down from the top of the rocks.

Fantasyland

- Snow White's Scary Adventures

Hint 53: The loading area mural shows the Dwarves' laundry hanging on a line. On the left side of a pair of boxer shorts (the

third pair from the right) is a red classic Mickey.

Hint 54: Below the bird and two flowers on the chimney in the loading area mural, three gray stones form a classic Mickey.

Hint 55: In the first part of the ride, the mirror that the Wicked Queen is looking into has three circles on top that form a classic Mickey.

Hint 56: Later in the ride, when you see the sign for the Dwarves' Mine, look closely to the right as your car curves to enter the mine. On the lower part of the right entrance panel, you'll see a drawing of Mickey (with a big nose) dressed as a Dwarf.

- Peter Pan's Flight

Hint 57: Close to the entrance turnstile, a group of trees faces the loading area. The fourth tree from the far end has a dark classic Mickey in the bark about halfway up the trunk.

Hint 58: As the ride begins, alphabet blocks on the floor to your right (and near Nana the dog) spell PPAN and DISNEY.

- The Many Adventures of Winnie the Pooh

Hint 59: At the beginning of the ride, in Rabbit's Garden, the small marker with radishes (in the middle pot to the left of the "Letus" sign) has one radish shaped like a classic Hidden Mickey.

Hint 60: At the beginning of the left wall of Owl's house (the second room on the ride) is a picture of Mr. Toad handing the deed to the house over to Owl (a tribute to the previous attraction in this building, Mr. Toad's Wild Ride).

Hint 61: Near the end of this room, on the right side of the floor, is another picture of Mr. Toad, this time standing with Winnie the Pooh.

Fantasyland, con't.

- Mickey's PhilHarmagic

Hint 62: In the first waiting area inside, the wall mural with musical instruments has several small white classic Mickeys.

Hint 63: On the right vertical border of the video screen in the main theater, a classic Mickey hides inside a French horn. (Thanks to D. Richmond for alerting me to this HM.)

- Pinocchio Village Haus Restaurant

Hint 64: As you head from the dining area to the restrooms, a tiny classic Mickey appears above the word "dreams" on the left wall near the exit to the restrooms.

- Cinderella's Royal Table Restaurant

Hint 65: Classic Mickeys are in the woodwork on the ceiling, near the flags.

- Fairytale Garden

Hint 66: At the base of the first light column on the right as you enter, a classic Mickey impression is in the cement on the side next to the fence. (Thanks to Lou Mongello for finding this HM.)

Hint 67: A side profile of Pluto's head is on the wall, upper left of the stage. It's left of the brick circle and above the stairs. (Thanks to my neighbor, Bob Ondercik, for spotting this one.)

- "it's a small world"

Hint 68: Toward the end of the Africa room, a vine on the right above the giraffes has purple leaves shaped like classic Mickey heads.

Hint 69: In the last room with the South Pacific theme, a clown with a "HELP" sign in a balloon has hair arranged so that his

head resembles a classic Mickey.

Hint 70: Below the flashing circle of lights on the right wall along the up-ramp exit is a flower with a purple center and circles that form a classic Mickey.

- Near *Peter Pan's Flight*

Hint 71: At the lower right of the entrance sign cloud formation is an incomplete classic cloud Mickey. It's just to the right of the "t."

Hint 72: Between *Peter Pan's Flight* and the restrooms nearby, next to Liberty Square, you'll find paintings of grape clusters on the walls. The lower three grapes in the second cluster from the right at the bottom resemble a classic Mickey.

Liberty Square

- Outside The Yankee Trader shop

Hint 73: A classic Mickey with hoofprints for ears and a water utility cover for a head can be found in the cement equidistant between The Yankee Trader shop and the Columbia Harbour House Restaurant, near the red cement.

Adventureland

- "The Enchanted Tiki Room Under New Management"

Hint 74: Upside-down classic Mickeys are camouflaged in the designs at the bottom of two bird perches. One perch is in the left corner as you enter the theater. The other is to the right of the exit door.

- *Jungle Cruise*

Hint 75: A giant spider, to the right of the treasure in the Cambodian Temple ruins, has three yellow circles on its back that form a classic Mickey.

41

Hint 76: The first undecorated column on the left wall (the third column from the end as you come out of the temple), has a chipped area of brick on the second block from the top. The chipped area forms part of a profile view of Mickey's head and face. Don't get discouraged if you have trouble spotting it; this is tough to find — especially the first time.

Tomorrowland

- Tomorrowland Transit Authority

Hint 77: The woman getting her hair done sports a belt buckle with a classic Hidden Mickey.

- Merchant of Venus Shop

Hint 78: In an outside display window, a dog with a rocket on his back wears a dogtag shaped like a classic Mickey.

- Mickey's Star Traders Shop

Hint 79: On the wall mural, the headlights of a train form a classic Mickey.

Hint 80: Stitch is racing beside a train in the mural.

Hint 81: Mickey hats sit atop windows halfway up the sides of a building.

Hint 82: Satellite dishes form a classic Mickey on top of this building.

Hint 83: Across the room on another wall mural, the middle circle of freeway loops forms a classic Mickey.

Hint 84: The large blue glass dome covering one building is a classic Mickey with ears.

Main Street, U.S.A.

Hint 85: In the Emporium store, metal poles that hold up merchandise shelves sport classic Mickey holes.

Hint 86: Candy bins in the Main Street Confectionary move along a track suspended from the ceiling. On the lower front and back sides of the bins are holes arranged like classic Mickeys.

Hint 87: The sign on the Caffe Italiano coffee cart, which is present seasonally in front of Tony's Town Square Restaurant, includes a classic Mickey in its design.

Hint 88: To the right of the entrance to Tony's Town Square Restaurant, the nose and eyes of the Goofy Pose-A-Matic device form a classic Mickey. (Thanks to my son Steven for spotting this Hidden Mickey.)

- From the WDW Railroad

Hint 89: In the riverboat scene near the end of the *Splash Mountain* ride, the upper outline of one of the white clouds on the right is shaped like Mickey Mouse lying on his back, his head to the right. This Hidden Mickey is also visible from the *Splash Mountain* ride (see Hint 8).

Epcot
Scavenger Hunt

• •

Many of the Hidden Mickeys in this park are in restaurants and shops. Be considerate of fellow guests and cast members as you search. Tell them what you're looking for, so they can share in the fun. Avoid searching restaurants at busy meal times unless you are one of the diners.

Note: I start the Epcot Scavenger Hunt in *Test Track* and *Mission: SPACE*. If you arrive early in the day, as I recommend, ask a "cast member" (Disney employee) if they are open. If not, do the *Living with the Land* ride (Clues 53 to 55) first and come back to *Test Track* and *Mission: SPACE*.

★ Go to the walkway through Innoventions East Side and get a FASTPASS for *Mission: SPACE*. Start your hunt in the **Test Track** waiting queue. Four Hidden Mickeys wait to be found.

(Try the singles line if the wait for *Test Track* is too long. FASTPASS is not an option here because some of the Mickeys in the entrance queue are hard to see from the FASTPASS line.)

Clue 1: Look for a Hidden Mickey among the objects on a tool chest.
3 points

Clue 2: Just before you get to the pre-show room, check the "Crash Test Vehicle" in area 5b very carefully.
2 points

★ Find two more Mickeys near the knee calibration area. Tip: The two are on the same desk exhibit.

Clue 3: Search out a classic Hidden Mickey.
2 points

45

Clue 4: Then find a Mickey Mouse doll.
2 points

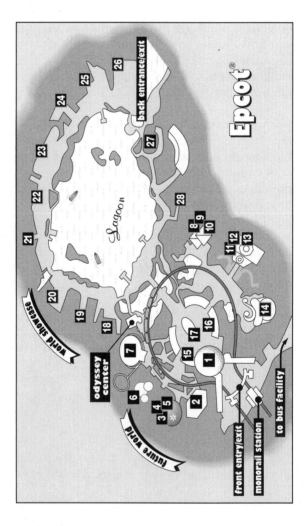

FUTURE WORLD

1. Spaceship Earth Pavilion
2. Universe of Energy Pavilion

Wonders of Life Pavilion
3. Body Wars
4. Cranium Command
5. The Making of Me

6. Mission: SPACE Pavilion
7. Test Track Pavilion

Imagination! Pavilion
8. Honey, I Shrunk the Audience
9. Journey Into Imagination with Figment
10. ImageWorks

The Land Pavilion
11. Living with the Land
12. The Circle of Life
13. Soarin'

14. The Living Seas Pavilion
15. Innoventions East Side
16. Innoventions West Side
17. Innoventions Plaza

WORLD SHOWCASE

18. Mexico: El Rio del Tiempo
19. Norway: Maelstrom
20. China: Reflections of China
21. Germany
22. Italy
23. U.S.A.: The American Adventure Show
24. Japan
25. Morocco
26. France: Impressions de France
27. United Kingdom
28. Canada: O Canada!

47

★ During the *Test Track* ride, try to find seven classic Mickeys. (Keep your eyes peeled; four of them are hard to spot.)

Clue 5: Look for the Mickey Mouse pencil in the first "Environmental Test" office.
2 points

Clue 6: In this same office, locate a classic Mickey made by a red Magic Marker.
3 points

Clue 7: Spot a Mickey Mouse doll in the second "Environmental Test" office.
3 points

★ In the "Corrosion Chamber" (the second chamber in the "Environmental Test" area), look fast to the right, then to the left to spot two classic Mickeys in rust.

Clue 8: On the right, check a hanging car door.
4 points

Clue 9: On your left, look for a truck fender.
4 points

Clue 10: As you approach the crash barrier wall, try to spot the classic Mickey crash test sticker on a white car to the left of your ride vehicle.
4 points

Clue 11: Then just before you reach the crash barrier wall, look at the floor to your left for one more.
4 points

Clue 12: After the ride, check out the monitors in the photo selection area for another look at the classic Mickey in Clue 11.
1 point

★ Go to **Mission: SPACE**. Ride the attraction to spot the first Hidden Mickey.

Clue 13: Just before launch, keep your eyes open for two identical Hidden Mickeys.
4 points

Clue 14: After the ride, look for a Hidden Mickey on a video console in the exhibit area.
2 points

Clue 15: Spot a Hidden Mickey on the ceiling of the gift shop at the attraction exit.
4 points

Clue 16: Squint for a small Hidden Mickey in a mural in the gift shop.
3 points

Clue 17: Find two classic Mickeys and a side profile Mickey on the wall of the gift shop.
2 points for all three

Clue 18: Outside in the front plaza, search for a classic Mickey on the moon.
3 points

★ Walk back to the Wonders of Life Pavilion. Go to **Body Wars**. Find the incredible Hidden Mickey in the mural above the entrance.

Clue 19: Check out the green "broccoli-like" tissue in the mural for a small side view of Mickey Mouse.
5 points

(This Hidden Mickey is a true classic! It's tough to spot the first time; so give yourself a big pat on the back when you find it.)

★ Watch the pre-show video to find two more Hidden Mickeys. Then ride *Body Wars* if you want (it's a simulator thrill ride), or skip it to look for more Hidden Mickeys.

Clue 20: During the pre-show video on the overhead monitors at the loading doors, look for two pictures of Mickey Mouse. (Tip: Both are on bags.)
2 points each

★ Visit **Cranium Command** next and look for three Hidden Mickeys.

Clue 21: In the waiting area, take a good

look at Walt Disney's brain.
1 point

Clue 22: In the main movie, look for the Hidden Mickey on the ceiling when the alarm clock awakens the boy.
5 points

Clue 23: Spot the classic Mickey on Principal Hardcase's desk lamp chain.
5 points

★ See **The Making of Me** and watch for two classic Mickeys.

Clue 24: Observe the balloons in the background during the school dance.
2 points

Clue 25: Take a good look at the mother's hospital gown.
2 points

★ Find three other Hidden Mickeys in the **Wonders of Life Pavilion**.

Clue 26: Observe the rotating red lights in the *Fitness Fairgrounds* area.
3 points

Clue 27: Hop aboard the *Wonder Cycle*. As you pedal your way to fitness, pay special attention to the Microworld program on your cycle's video screen. Can you spot the Mickey Mouse doll?
4 points

Tip: If the Microworld program isn't on the cycle when you start, just stop pedaling and the computer will jump to the next video. You may have to stop twice to get to it.

Clue 28: As you exit the Pavilion, gaze at the colorful mural on the wall for a classic Mickey.
3 points

★ When World Showcase opens, take the central walkway **from Future World, heading toward Norway.**

Clue 29: Turn left and search for a classic Mickey on a hot dog truck.
2 points

★ Go to **Maelstrom** in the Norway Pavilion. Study the loading area mural to find two Hidden Mickeys. Enjoy the ride and movie if you wish. (If there are Hidden Mickeys to be found in either, I haven't yet spotted them.)

Clue 30: Find the Viking wearing Mickey ears.
3 points

Clue 31: Look for the flight attendant with Mickey's face outlined in the creases of her shirt. (This is a hard one to spot.)
4 points

★ Eat an early lunch to avoid the crowds. The San Angel Inn Restaurant is an ideal choice if you have 11:30 a.m. or so priority seating reservations. If not, try fast food at Cantina de San Angel at the Mexico Pavilion. Or try to get seated at Restaurant Akershus in Norway (if you like seafood); it sometimes has tables available.

★ If you eat in the **San Angel Inn**, look for classic Mickeys in the smoke rising from the volcano (see Clue and Hint 35).

★ Go to **El Rio del Tiempo** in the Mexico Pavilion and keep your eyes peeled for classic Mickeys.

Clue 32: At the beginning of the ride, take a close look at the smoke rising from the volcano.
4 points

Clue 33: In a street market scene toward the end of the ride, find the classic Mickey formed by three pots on the ground.
3 points

Clue 34: Near the end of the ride, spot the small white statue and the Hidden Mickey shadow it casts.
2 points

★ After exiting the ride, walk to the **San Angel Inn Restaurant** (if you haven't already been there) and look for classic Mickeys that appear and disappear.

Clue 35: Observe the smoke rising from the volcano. Ask the attendants to let you walk to the fence by the river if you need a closer look.
4 points

★ Walk left to **Germany** and find two Hidden Mickeys.

Clue 36: As you walk into the plaza, look for the classic Mickey on a suit of armor on the building to your right.
3 points

Clue 37: Outside in the miniature train exhibit, locate the Hidden Mickeys on a church.
3 points

★ Now check out the rest of the landscaping around the train attraction to earn some possible bonus points. 1 point for each Hidden Mickey you spot.
(These Hidden Mickeys come and go.)

★ Go to the **U.S.A. Pavilion** and check out the rear wall of the rotunda, upstairs and down, for classic Hidden Mickeys.

Clue 38: Take a good look at the bronze eagle reliefs.
2 points for each floor

★ Now watch **The American Adventure Show** and keep an eye out for two hard-to-spot classic Hidden Mickeys.

Clue 39: At the beginning of the film, look at the rocks behind a kneeling female pilgrim.
4 points

Clue 40: At the end, watch the fireworks explosions behind the Statue of Liberty Torch.
5 points

★ Stroll over to **Japan**.

Clue 41: Look up at the small holes on the gold ornaments hanging from the corners of the pagoda.
3 points

Clue 42: Search for a classic Mickey in the koi fish pond.
2 points

Clue 43: Check out the grates at the base of the trees in the courtyard.
2 points

★ Meander to **Morocco**.

Clue 44: Gaze at the promenade shop exterior.
2 points

★ Go to **France**.

Clue 45: Examine the grates at the base of the trees in the courtyard.
2 points

Clue 46: Find the classic Mickey bush on the right side of the ornamental garden.
3 points

Clue 47: In the movie **Impressions de France**, spot Mickey's head and ears in the background of the wedding scene.
4 points

★ Go to the International Gateway entrance turnstiles at **Epcot's rear entrance** and check the time.

Clue 48: Take a good look at the clock tower.
2 points

★ Enter the **United Kingdom**.

Clue 49: Gaze at a classic sports Mickey from the street.
2 points

★ Walk over to **Canada** to find more classic Mickeys.

Clue 50: Examine the totem pole on the left near the steps into the pavilion.
3 points

★ Return to Future World and walk to Ice Station Cool at the end of Innoventions West Side. Enjoy free exotic and refreshing soft drinks from foreign countries.

★ Get a FASTPASS for the *Living with the Land* ride in the Land Pavilion. Then cross back through the Innoventions buildings to the **Universe of Energy**. Find a Hidden Mickey as you take in the show and ride.

Clue 51: After the dinosaur section of the ride, watch the movie and look for the shadow of the Disney-MGM Studios "Earffel" Tower (the tower with Mickey ears) in the door of a church in the background.
5 points

★ Cross back again to **The Living Seas Pavilion** and find a coral classic Mickey in Sea Base Alpha.

Clue 52: Look through the aquarium window that is second nearest to the restrooms.
4 points

★ Head right to the **Living with the Land** ride at your FASTPASS time. Study the wall murals to find two classic Hidden Mickeys.

Clue 53: Take a good look at the bubbles in the mural at the rear of the entrance queue.
3 points

Clue 54: Now check the lower part of the mural behind the loading area.
3 points

Clue 55: Toward the end of the ride, find the green Hid-den Mickey in the round test tube holder in a lab room.
3 points

★ Go inside the **Garden Grill Restaurant** upstairs and take a good look at the back wall.

Clue 56: Notice the sunflowers.
1 point

Clue 57: Find and then marvel at the green face of Mickey Mouse on the left side of the large wall mural of vegetation. He's in three-quarter profile and well camouflaged by the leaves of a single fern. Counting up horizontally from the bottom of the fern, his face is mostly behind the fifth through eighth leaves on the fern's right side.
5 points

★ Go to the railing in front of the entrance to **The Circle of Life** movie to spot a classic Mickey.

Clue 58: Focus on the side of one of the balloons.
3 points

★ Keep your priority seating reservations for dinner. If you don't have reservations, eat at the Food Court in the Land Pavilion.

★ Go to the Imagination! Pavilion and ride **Journey Into Imagination with Figment**.

Clue 59: Squint for a black classic Mickey in the Sight Room.
4 points

Clue 60: Look for a classic Mickey on the wall along the exit hallway.
3 points

★ Cross through Innoventions West Side and head for **Spaceship Earth**. Line up for the ride.

Clue 61: See if you can find the rocket with Mickey ears in its identification number. Tip: The rocket is in the mural.
2 points

Clue 62: During the ride, notice the Hidden Mickey on the document in front of the sleeping monk.
4 points

Clue 63: In the Renaissance section, spot the classic Mickey formed by paint circles on a tabletop near a painter. Psst! Look quickly to your left.
3 points

Clue 64: In the teenage boy's bedroom, check out the baseball cap.
2 points

Clue 65: Then take a good look at the alarm clock.
2 points

★ Walk to the **Tip Board** in Innoventions Plaza.

Clue 66: Look carefully at the continents on the rotating earth that forms the "O" in Epcot.
3 points

★ Walk inside **Innoventions East**.

Clue 67: Spot a classic Mickey on the wall.
2 points

★ Go to the **Mouse Gear Shop** in Innoventions East, where you'll find a number of Hidden Mickeys and décor Mickeys.

Clue 68: Before you enter, find the classic Mickey in the sign above the shop entrance.
1 point

★ Now step inside and keep your eyes peeled.

Clue 69: Examine the nuts on the display racks' bolts.
1 point

Clue 70: Then look for classic Mickeys at the ends of the display racks.
1 point

Clue 71: Now check out the bolt ends themselves.
2 points

Clue 72: Examine the bottom supports for the display racks. (They aren't all the same.)
2 points

Clue 73: Observe the gauges on the wall.
1 point

Clue 74: Finally, look at the tops of the garment display mannequins.
1 point

Total Points for Epcot =

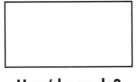

How'd you do?
Up to 84 points - Bronze
85 - 169 points - Silver
170 points and over - Gold
213 points - Perfect Score

(If you earned bonus points outside the miniature train exhibit in Germany,
you may have done even better!)

Notes

HINTS HINTS HINTS HINTS HINTS HINTS HINTS HINTS HINTS HINTS HINTS HINTS HINTS HINTS HINTS

**Caution:
Don't peek at this
section unless you
really want help!**

Test Track

- in the waiting queue

Hint 1: Across from area 10a, look for a red tool cabinet. A mug on top of it has a Pez dispenser with a Mickey Mouse head.

Hint 2: As the queue lines climb toward the pre-show room (and before you get to it), a white "Crash Test Vehicle" in area 5b sports a small inspection sticker. (It's visible from the left queue.) The sticker, signed by "M. Mouse," is on the front passenger door.

Hint 3: Near knee calibration area 7b, on the left side of the queue, three washers at the edge of a desk (left of center of the desktop) form an upside-down classic Mickey.

Hint 4: A Mickey Mouse doll sits on an upper shelf at the right side of the same desk.

59

- during the ride

Hint 5: During the "Environmental Test" part of the ride, in the second window of the first office to the right of the ride vehicle, a cup contains a pencil with a classic Mickey outline at the top.

Hint 6: In the first "Environmental Test" office, a classic Mickey drawn with a red Magic Marker appears on the upper part of a grease board on the rear wall.

Hint 7: In the second window of the second "Environmental Test" office to the right of the ride vehicle, a Mickey Mouse plush doll is sitting with its back against the window. (Thanks to my sister Donna for finding this HM.)

Hints 8 & 9: You have to look quickly to the right, then the left as you enter the "Corrosion Chamber" to spot two classic Mickeys on auto parts that are just inside the room. Look for a hanging car door to the right and a truck fender to the left. Both sport classic Mickey rust spots.

Hint 10: As you approach the crash barrier wall, a white car (to the left and facing the ride vehicle) has a classic Mickey on its open gas tank door. It is formed by three crash test stickers.

Hint 11: Just before the crash barrier wall, look to the floor on your left to try to spot hoses coiled to form a classic Mickey.

This Hidden Mickey is hard to spot because you are moving so fast. But you can see it on the *Test Track* photo monitors (see below) if you miss it during the ride.

- after the ride

Hint 12: At the *Test Track* photo selection area, check the monitors to see the hoses coiled like classic Mickeys. You'll find them in the upper right area of the photos.

Mission: SPACE

Hint 13: You'll see identical classic Hidden

Mickeys above a horizontal bar on both sides of the launch door before it opens and before you see the sky.

Hint 14: In the Expedition Mars section of the exit-exhibit area, you'll find small classic Mickeys in the design of the video game joystick consoles at the upper left and upper right corners.

Hint 15: In the center of the gift shop near the exit doors, a large side profile of Mickey Mouse is painted on the ceiling in the middle square.

Hint 16: In the mural behind the gift shop's cash register, look for Minnie Mouse. There's a small classic Mickey in the ground under her left foot.

Hint 17: On both sides of the exit door from the gift shop, you'll find two classic Mickeys and a side profile Mickey in the electrical tubing on the wall.

Hint 18: Three craters that approximate a classic Mickey are at the upper left of the Luna 8 landing site on the back side of the moon. (Thanks to my friend John Perry for spotting this HM.)

Wonders of Life Pavilion

- Body Wars

Hint 19: In the mural above the entrance is a small side view of Mickey Mouse, who is gazing toward the upper left of the mural. He is in the right-most green "broccoli-like" tissue.

Hint 20: In the pre-show video, look for a woman walking to her seat carrying a shopping bag and a person stowing a paper bag under the seat. Both bags are decorated with a picture of Mickey Mouse.

- Cranium Command

Hint 21: On the waiting area wall, a "Hall of Brains" poster sports a picture of Walt Disney's brain with a classic Mickey on it.

HINTS HINTS HINTS HINTS HINTS HINTS HINTS HINTS HINTS HINTS HINTS HINTS HINTS

Hint 22: At the beginning of the main movie, the alarm clock awakens the boy, who looks up at the ceiling. To the right of the suspended airplanes is a faint, dark frontal profile of Mickey Mouse's body.

Hint 23: At the end of the chain on Principal Hardcase's desk lamp is an upside-down classic Mickey.

- The Making of Me

Hint 24: During the school dance, the pink and blue balloons in the background come together to form classic Mickeys.

Hint 25: The mother's hospital gown is patterned with classic Hidden Mickeys.

- Fitness Fairgrounds

Hint 26: Rotating red lights in the *Fitness Fairgrounds* area repeatedly form classic Mickeys. You can see them from the *Cranium Command* exit area.

- Wonder Cycle

Hint 27: In the *Wonder Cycle's* Microworld program, a Mickey Mouse plush doll is in the bedroom of a house at the upper part of the cycle's video screen.

Hint 28: A classic Mickey with an orange circle for the head and two red circles for ears can be found in the colorful mural on the wall as you exit the Pavilion. (Thanks to J. Baublitz for showing this one to me.)

World Showcase

- heading toward Norway from Future World

Hint 29: A "Tasty Treats" hot dog truck sits outside a shop between the central walkway and the Mexico Pavilion. You'll find a classic Mickey on the top middle of the truck's radiator grill. (Thanks to G. Rose for this one.)

Norway Pavilion

- *Maelstrom*

Hint 30: On the left side of the large loading-area mural, a Viking in a ship wears Mickey ears.

Hint 31: Toward the right side of the same mural, a woman flight attendant holds a clipboard. To the left of the top of her clipboard, the creases in her white shirt form a side profile of Mickey's face. His face is slightly distorted and he's looking to your left.

Mexico Pavilion

- *El Rio del Tiempo*

Hint 32: At the beginning of the boat ride, smoke rises from the volcano. Every half minute or so, it forms classic Mickeys that quickly disappear.

Hint 33: Toward the end of the boat ride, the video displays three street-market scenes (off to your left). At the end of the second scene (between the second and third arches), look for three pots on the ground. They form a classic Hidden Mickey.

Hint 34: On the left side of the boat, near the end of the ride, a small white statue casts a classic Mickey shadow on the wall. Look in front and to the far right of the Mexico wall map.

- *San Angel Inn Restaurant*

Hint 35: Smoke rising from the volcano by the river forms classic Mickeys that quickly disappear.

Germany Pavilion

Hint 36: On the second floor of the building to your right, to the right of the glockenspiel clock, are three suits of armor. The one closest to the glockenspiel has a classic Mickey on its crown.

- around the Miniature Train exhibit

Hint 37: Look for Mickey's head in the middle of the front section of the exhibit. Tiny brown Hidden Mickeys (just the top of his head with his ears) can be found in both the frieze above the church entrance door that faces the small plaza and above the small windows at the rear of the church.

U.S.A. Pavilion

Hint 38: On the rear wall of the rotunda, first and second floors, large bronze eagle reliefs have classic Mickeys in the corners.

- The American Adventure Show

Hint 39: At the beginning of the film, a classic Mickey appears on the rock behind and to your right of a kneeling female pilgrim.

Hint 40: At the end of the show, fireworks light up the sky behind the Statue of Liberty Torch as it rises from the floor. One of the fireworks at the upper right fizzles into a classic Mickey head (best seen from the right side of the theater).

Japan Pavilion

Hint 41: Each gold ornament hanging from the corners of the pagoda has small classic Mickey holes along the bottom edge of the upper bell. (Thanks to my neighbor, Karen Taylor, for finding this Hidden Mickey jewel!)

Hint 42: In the koi fish pond across from the Mitsukoshi Store, a drain cover in the water near the bamboo fence sports a classic Mickey. (Thanks to my sister Donna for telling me about this one.)

Hint 43: The trees in the courtyard are encircled by metal grates with classic Mickey designs.

Morocco Pavilion

Hint 44: Three brass plates are arranged

to form a classic Mickey on the left green door at the entrance to the Souk-Al-Magreb "Gifts of Morocco" shop on the promenade.

France Pavilion

Hint 45: Here again, the trees in the courtyard are encircled by metal grates with classic Mickey patterns.

Hint 46: In the patterned hedge (parterre) garden, a bush in the middle right area (on the side nearest the canal) is trimmed to the shape of a classic Mickey.

- Impressions de France

Hint 47: In the movie's outdoor wedding scene, you can see a Mickey head and ears in a second floor window, center screen, of the house in the background.

Rear Entrance Clock Tower

Hint 48: On the clock tower adjacent to the entrance turnstiles, the clock face and the scrollwork underneath together form an upside-down classic Mickey.

United Kingdom Pavilion

Hint 49: Outside the Sportsman's Shoppe, a sign has a classic Mickey with a tennis racket head, a soccer ball for one ear and a rugby ball for the other.

Canada Pavilion

Hint 50: Past the steps into the pavilion, the left totem pole has black classic Mickeys on both sides near the top by the raven's beak.

Universe of Energy

Hint 51: After the dinosaur section of the ride, the movie shows a man driving a car out of a barn and past a church building in the background. A shadow of the Disney-MGM Studios "Earffel" Tower appears in the door of the church.

The Living Seas Pavilion

Hint 52: In the aquarium, coral with reddish-brown spots forms a classic Mickey. To find it, go to the restrooms in Sea Base Alpha, then walk to the second window from the restrooms. You'll spot the coral near the top of the middle rock.

The Land Pavilion

- Living with the Land

Hint 53: In the middle section of the giant wall mural at the rear of the queue, bubbles align to form a classic Mickey, ears angled to the left.

Hint 54: In the lower right area of the mural behind the boat loading area, three circles form a small classic Mickey (a green circle for the head and blue circles for the ears). The head is tilted slightly to the right.

Hint 55: Toward the end of the ride, a large circular test tube holder on the right side of a laboratory room has a green classic Mickey head in the center.

- Garden Grill Restaurant

Hint 56: Some of the sunflowers along the lower edge of the smaller sunflower field that's painted on the back wall form classic Mickeys.

Hint 57: On the left side of the large wall mural of vegetation is a Mickey hiding behind the most prominent fern that extends all the way to the top. He's looking slightly downward and to the right in a three-quarter profile. Two black circles that form his eyes are visible above the sixth fern leaf on the right, more than halfway to the end of the leaf. Mickey's ears jut above the seventh leaf, and his mouth and nose are below the sixth leaf. His face and ears are green, and his mouth is slightly open. This Hidden Mickey is a real classic!

66

- The Circle of Life Entrance

Hint 58: Reddish circles on the side of the large green balloon suspended from the pavilion ceiling form a classic Mickey head.

Imagination! Pavilion

- Journey Into Imagination with Figment

Hint 59: In the Sight Room, a poster below the words "focus Group" has a tiny classic Mickey in the left lower corner..

Hint 60: On the left wall of the exit hallway, a sideways classic Mickey is behind and between the "I" and "m" of the "ImageWorks" sign.

Spaceship Earth

Hint 61: The mural to the right of the entrance walkway includes a rocket with an ID number on its side. You'll find Mickey's ears inside the circles of the number "3."

Hint 62: During the ride, in a scene to the left, monks are writing at desks. In front of the sleeping monk is a document with a small ink blot at the upper right corner. The blot is shaped like a classic Mickey and becomes visible as your vehicle passes by.

Hint 63: Just after the Gutenberg printing press scene, in the first part of the Renaissance section, look for the first painter to the left of your ride vehicle. Three white paint circles form a classic Mickey on the top left of the table near the painter. You have to look fast for this one.

Hint 64: In the teenage boy's bedroom, a baseball cap hanging from a wall hook sports a big M for Mickey.

Hint 65: Mickey is also on the alarm clock on the boy's dresser.

Tip Board in Innoventions Plaza

Hint 66: Australia is shaped like a classic Mickey on the rotating earth that forms the "O" in Epcot.

Innoventions East

Hint 67: On the wall maps inside the various entrance doors, a classic Mickey computer mouse is the icon for area number 9.

- Mouse Gear Shop

Hint 68: The signs above the shop entrances have classic Mickeys with two round ears above the letter "G" as the head.

Hint 69: The large wing nuts on the bolts of the display racks form Mickey ears.

Hint 70: At the ends of some of the display racks, bolts next to larger holes form classic Mickeys.

Hint 71: The ends of some of the large bolts are stamped with classic Mickeys.

Hint 72: The bottom supports for some of the display racks are gears arranged as classic Mickeys.

Hint 73: Some of the gauges on the wall are arranged as classic Mickeys.

Hint 74: Some of the garment display mannequins have classic Mickeys at the top.

CHAPTER 4

Disney MGM Studios Scavenger Hunt

••••••••••••••••••••••••••••

Note: Many of the Hidden Mickeys in this park are in restaurants and shops. Be considerate of fellow guests and cast members as you search. Tell them what you're looking for, so they can share in the fun. Avoid searching restaurants at busy meal times unless you are one of the diners.

★ Your scavenger hunt in Disney-MGM Studios (aka, "the Studios") starts even **before you enter** the park.

Clue 1: Look closely at the brackets on the signs above the ticket windows.
2 points

Clue 2: Examine the fence at the entrance turnstiles.
1 point

★ Now go to **Rock 'n' Roller Coaster Starring Aerosmith**.

(You can find the Hidden Mickeys here without riding the coaster, the first by exiting before the ride and the second by walking in through the exit from outside.)

Clue 3: At the loading gate, look at the rear license plates of the limo ride vehicles. (Then exit if you wish.)
4 points

Clue 4: At the exit, find a box with a classic Mickey.
4 points

★ Walk to **The Twilight Zone Tower of Terror** and explore the entry queue area and pre-show for four Hidden Mickeys.

(You can exit before the ride if you want; you won't miss any Hidden Mickeys.)

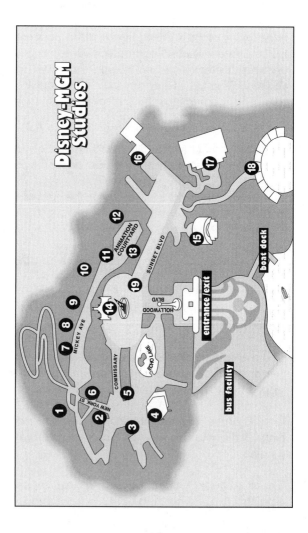

Disney-MGM Studios

1. Lights, Motors, Action! Extreme Stunt Show
2. Jim Henson's MuppetVision 3D
3. Star Tours
4. Indiana Jones™ Epic Stunt Spectacular
5. Sounds Dangerous — Starring Drew Carey
6. "Honey, I Shrunk the Kids" Movie Set Adventure
7. Disney-MGM Studios Backlot Tour
8. Backstage Pass (closed as we go to press)
9. Who Wants to Be a Millionaire — Play It!
10. Walt Disney: One Man's Dream
11. Voyage of The Little Mermaid
12. The Magic of Disney Animation
13. Playhouse Disney — Live on Stage!
14. The Great Movie Ride
15. Beauty and the Beast
16. Rock 'n' Roller Coaster Starring Aerosmith
17. The Twilight Zone Tower of Terror™
18. Fantasmic!
19. Guest Information Board

Clue 5: Along the entry queue, just past the entrance to the hotel lobby, find the wire-rimmed glasses that form a classic Mickey.
2 points

Clue 6: During the pre-show film in the library, find the plush Mickey Mouse doll held by a little girl.
3 points

Clue 7: Linger in the left library to spot the words "Mickey Mouse" on sheet music on the bookcase.
4 points

Clue 8: Notice a classic Mickey stain on the wall in the boiler room.
4 points

★ Head down Sunset Boulevard and through the arch to get in line for the first show of **Voyage of The Little Mermaid** (or return later if you missed the first show and the next is more than an hour away).

If you have more than 30 minutes until show time, you may want to look for some of the Hidden Mickeys on Sunset and Hollywood Boulevards while you wait (see below, Clues 30 to 32 and 47 to 53). Plan to be back 15 to 20 minutes before the show starts (or 30 to 40 minutes ahead if you are seeing a later show). Or get a FASTPASS.

Clue 9: As the show starts, watch the laser lights near the ceiling and find a Hidden Mickey.
3 points

★ Walk back through the arch and turn right to **The Great Movie Ride**. First find two classic Mickeys among the celebrity impressions in the cement in front of the Chinese Theater and then take the ride.

(If the wait is more than 15 minutes, go on to *Who Wants to Be a Millionaire—Play It!* or *Star Tours* and try this later. Best times: during a parade or two hours before park closing.)

72

Clue 10: Check Harry Anderson's square.
3 points

Clue 11: Now spot a Mickey in Carol Burnett's square.
3 points

Clue 12: In the middle of the loading dock mural, search for the Hidden Minnie above a tree stump. Tip: It's visible at loading and unloading.
5 points

Clue 13: As you start down Gangster Alley, look for Mickey's brown shoes under a James Cagney poster.
4 points

Clue 14: At the end of Gangster Alley, find Mickey's shadow in a window near the top of the "Chemical Company" building.
5 points

Clue 15: Find Mickey and Donald on the left wall, at the end of the "Raiders of the Lost Ark" scene. Psst! Mickey is facing Donald.
5 points

★ Exit and cross Mickey Avenue to **Who Wants to Be a Millionaire – Play It!** Get in line or get a FASTPASS to return later if the wait is too long.

Clue 16: As you exit the show, look for the fire extinguisher box sporting a Hidden Mickey.
2 points

★ Turn left at the exit, walk past the Sorcerer's hat and across the park (with Echo Lake on your left) to **Star Tours**. Catch two Hidden characters along the entrance queue and another in the pre-boarding instructional video. You can exit before the ride if you prefer to focus on the scavenger hunt.

(If the line is too long, use the FASTPASS option if it's available to you. If you're holding a FASTPASS for Millionaire and aren't yet eligible for another, return after lunch and either ride *Star Tours* or get a FAST-PASS for it. You should be eligible for one by then.)

Clue 17: Marvel at a Hidden Kermit the Frog on the right side of the entrance queue.
4 points

Clue 18: Spot a classic Mickey metal disk moving along a track above you in the entrance queue.
4 points

Clue 19: Keep an eye out for an Ewok taking his seat in the *Star Tours* instructional video.
2 points

★ Take a lunch break. Keep your priority seating reservations if you have them. If not, try the Backlot Express for burgers and sandwiches, the Toy Story Pizza Planet for pizza, or the ABC Commissary for salads and stir-fry.

★ After lunch, go to *Jim Henson's MuppetVision 3-D* and find five Hidden Mickeys.

Clue 20: Look for a Mickey Mouse in the fountain outside MuppetVision.
2 points

Clue 21: On the wall near the far turn of the long outside waiting queue, check out the poster about 3-D glasses to find a classic Mickey.
3 points

Clue 22: Observe the test pattern during the first part of the pre-show on the video monitors.
4 points

Clue 23: Near the end of the main show, find the classic Mickey on band members' Colonial-style hats.
4 points

Clue 24: Try to spot the Mickey balloons after Kermit rides in on a fire truck.
3 points

★ Walk up New York Street. Turn right and pass by the *Honey I Shrunk the Kids Movie Set Adventure* to *The Disney-MGM Studios Backlot Tour*. Find three classic Mickeys as you tour.

Clue 25: In the background mural at the special effects water tank, find a blue clas-

sic Mickey in the clouds.
5 points

Clue 26: Look closely at the refrigerator on the right side of the first aisle in the prop storage area.
3 points

Caution: If the waiting queue is short, you may bypass the winding aisles. If you do, look down the first aisle to spot the fridge.

Clue 27: Just after the "Shangri La" airplane and before Catastrophe Canyon, look to the right for a classic Mickey on a white box. (The box is visible again, to your left, after you exit Catastrophe Canyon.)
3 points

★ Turn left down **Mickey Avenue** to the "Disney Stars" trailer across from the "Stage 1" sign.

Clue 28: Find two classic Mickeys on the trailer.
3 points for both

★ Continue down Mickey Avenue, then up the steps or through the arch, and veer left to enter **The Hollywood Brown Derby** restaurant. Look at the pictures in the waiting area.

Clue 29: Spot the man with Mickey Mouse ears.
3 points

★ Turn left as you leave, and head down **Sunset Boulevard**. Wander into **Planet Hollywood Super Store** and gaze at the amber block on the wall.

Clue 30: Find a classic Mickey in the area near the mosquito.
4 points

★ Turn left onto Hollywood Boulevard, then right to enter **Hollywood & Vine restaurant**. Examine the left wall.

Clue 31: Find a stick figure Mickey.
2 points

★ Step inside the waiting area for the **50's Prime Time Café** and look closely at the tables.

Clue 32: Check what's holding them together.
1 point

★ Stroll to the **Radio Disney sign** to the left of *Sounds Dangerous.*

Clue 33: Take a good look at the "O."
1 point

★ Ask a restaurant cast member to let you check out the inside of the **Sci-Fi Dine-In Theater Restaurant**.

Clue 34: Examine the right rear mural. Look for a classic Mickey head in a tree above the tall fence.
5 points

Clue 35: Watch the movie reel for a Hidden character.
5 points

★ Get some coffee or other refreshment at **The Writer's Stop**. Look up while you are enjoying it.

Clue 36: See anything on the overhead theater lights?
2 points

★ Mosey over to the **Toy Story Pizza Planet** and find three Hidden Mickeys.

Clue 37: Search for a small classic Mickey in the stars above the counter registers. Focus on the left side of the pizzeria's rear wall.
4 points

Clue 38: Swing your eyes over to the right side of the rear wall to find a bright classic-Mickey star.
3 points

Clue 39: Now find a three-quarter Mickey profile above the arcade games on the wall mural. Psst! He's looking left.
5 points

★ Wander into the **Stage 1 Company**

Store and find two Hidden Mickeys.

Clue 40: Take a good look at the old bureau that's loaded with hats and paint cans.
3 points

Clue 41: Search for some famous shorts.
3 points

★ In the waiting area for **Mama Melrose's Ristorante Italiano**, search for four classic Mickeys.

Clue 42: Check the Dalmatian.
3 points

Clue 43: Examine the plaster on the right wall.
4 points

Clue 44: Find a classic Mickey leaf near the check-in podium.
4 points

Clue 45: Now look at the plaster on the wall to the left of the check-in podium.
4 points

★ Walk down **New York Street**.

Clue 46: Admire the paintings in a window near the end of the street.
4 points

★ Walk left to Commissary Lane, then on to Hollywood Boulevard. At the **intersection of Hollywood and Sunset** Boulevards, discover Mickey Mouse's previous moniker.

Clue 47: Read the impressions in the sidewalks, near the curb.
5 points

★ Look at a billboard above the **Keystone Clothiers** shop.

Clue 48: See any handprints in cement?
3 points

★ Enter **Mickey's of Hollywood** store to look for four Hidden Mickeys.

Clue 49: Check the posts holding up the merchandise racks.
2 points

Clue 50: Now examine the racks themselves.
2 points

Clue 51: Study the cabinets in the Sorcerer section of the store. Tip: They are near a door to the street.
2 points

Clue 52: Find "MICKEY" spelled out on vertical dividers.
1 point

★ Go to the **Cover Story Store** and take a good look at the outside.

Clue 53: Can you spot the classic Mickeys in the design?
2 points

Clue 54: Turn the **Disney-MGM Studios park map** upside down and search for Mickey.
4 points

Clue 55: In the **Fantasmic!** show, look for large bubbles floating up the water screen that form a classic Hidden Mickey.
4 points

Total Points for Disney-MGM Studios =

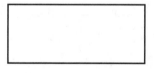

How'd you do?
Up to 71 points - Bronze
72 - 142 points - Silver
143 points and over - Gold
179 points - Perfect Score

**Caution:
Don't peek at this
section unless you
really want help!**

- Park entrance area

Hint 1: Metal brackets at the bottom of signs above the ticket purchase windows are shaped like classic Mickeys.

Hint 2: You'll see classic Mickeys on the top of the fence.

- Rock 'n' Roller Coaster Starring Aerosmith

Hint 3: On the rear license plate of each limo ride vehicle, the year sticker at the upper right is a classic Mickey.

Hint 4: Just as people exit the ride vehicle, look for "Box #15" on the side. The "o" in "Box" is a classic Mickey. (Thanks to A. O'Neill for telling me about this HM.)

- The Twilight Zone Tower of Terror

79

Hint 5: Just past the entrance to the hotel lobby, observe the wire-rimmed glasses on a desk to the right. They're folded to form a classic Mickey.

Hint 6: During the pre-show film in the library, the little girl on the elevator holds a plush Mickey Mouse doll.

Hint 7: Look for sheet music on the bookcase in the left library. The words "Mickey Mouse" are included in a song title.

Hint 8: A black, slightly distorted classic Mickey is on the wall of the boiler room at the spot where the queue branches, about 8 feet up from the walkway, between an "Exit" sign and a red electrical box.

- Voyage of The Little Mermaid

Hint 9: At the beginning of the show, just after the words "Voyage of The Little Mermaid" appear on the screen, laser lights converge high up, near the ceiling, to form a classic Mickey.

- The Great Movie Ride

Hint 10: Harry Anderson's celebrity impression is at the front left of the Chinese Theater (as you face the entrance). Look for a classic Mickey on Harry's tie.

Hint 11: Four squares to the right of Harry Anderson's impression, Carol Burnett's square has a classic Mickey in the upper right side.

Hint 12: In the loading dock area, a shadow of Minnie Mouse's head in side profile is visible on the wall mural during loading and unloading. To find it, first spot the house in the middle of the mural. Then look above and to the right of the house to spot Minnie's shadow. She's looking to your left. Having trouble? Look at the ride vehicles. The shadow is to the left of the front section of the second of the two vehicles.

Hint 13: In the first part of Gangster Alley, Mickey Mouse's brown shoes poke out from under a James Cagney poster, "The

Public Enemy," on the left side of the ride vehicle.

Hint 14: At the end of Gangster Alley, a shadow of Mickey in side profile appears in the right-most window, near the top of the "Chemical Company" building. It's to the rear left of your ride vehicle.

Hint 15: On the upper part of the left wall, at the end of the "Raiders of the Lost Ark" scene, Mickey and Donald can be found in the far left corner of the scene. They're facing one another and Mickey is right of Donald.

- Who Wants To Be A Millionaire – Play It!

Hint 16: At the right side of the exit doors is a fire extinguisher box with a glass classic Mickey on its door.

- Star Tours

Hint 17: Along the entrance queue in the room with the moving baskets, wave at Kermit the Frog, who is made from tubes and extra robot parts. He is sitting on the right side of the lower ascending walkway, before it makes a sharp turn to the right.

Hint 18: Along this section of the entrance queue, take your time and study the moving baskets above you. In several of them, a metal disk shaped like a classic Mickey is propped upright. (Thanks to my friend John Weyrich for pointing out this Mickey.)

Hint 19: During the first part of the pre-boarding instructional video, an Ewok carries a plush Mickey Mouse as he moves across the row to his seat on the StarSpeeder. He places the doll under his seat.

- Jim Henson's MuppetVision 3-D

Hint 20: In a fountain outside the attraction, Gonzo is balancing on a character that resembles Mickey Mouse with bulging eyes.

Hint 21: On the wall near the far turn of the long out-side waiting queue, you'll find a classic Mickey in the center left of a blue poster that says, "5 reasons to re-turn . . . 3-D glasses."

Hint 22: During the first part of the pre-show on the video monitors, a test pattern appears. The black lines on a white background form a classic Hidden Mickey.

Hint 23: Near the end of the main show, during the Muppets' celebration with marching bands and fire-works, some of the band members wear blue Colo-nial-style hats with red tabs on the side. The tabs have classic Mickeys in the center.

Hint 24: After the cannon shoots holes in the theater and Kermit rides in on a fire truck, some of the ob-servers outside are holding Mickey balloons.

- Disney-MGM Studios Backlot Tour

Hint 25: In the background mural at the special ef-fects water tank, a blue classic Mickey appears in the clouds to the left of the light scaffolding. Scan down from the top of the mural and you'll find it about halfway down.

Hint 26: On the right side of the first aisle in the movie and TV prop storage area, the front of a yellow re-frigerator sports a silver classic Mickey.

Hint 27: Just after you pass the "Shangri La" airplane and before you enter Catastrophe Canyon, look to the right for a white box which sports a dark classic Mickey emblem. (If you miss it on the way in to the Canyon, you'll have another chance to spot it as you leave, because the road loops around. Look to your left just after you exit.)

- Mickey Avenue

Hint 28 A large black classic Mickey is on the "Disney Stars" trailer's hubcap and tiny

white classic Mickeys are scattered in the blue background on its side. (Thanks to the Buaas family for these HMs.)

- The Hollywood Brown Derby restaurant

Hint 29: On a wall to the left, in the second row of pictures, you'll find a caricature of Jimmy Dodd (with his Mouse ears) from the 1950s' "Mickey Mouse Club" TV show.

- Planet Hollywood Super Store

Hint 30: On an inside wall, to the left of the main entrance from Sunset Boulevard, you'll see an amber block with a trapped mosquito. The air bubbles in the upper left of the block form a classic Mickey.

- Hollywood & Vine restaurant

Hint 31: On the left wall, the "San Fernando Valley" wall mural has a stick figure Mickey on the far right, behind a pole.

- 50's Prime Time Café

Hint 32: In the waiting area, washers shaped like classic Mickeys secure the white tabletops.

- Radio Disney sign

Hint 33: The "O" in the Radio Disney sign has a classic Mickey in the center.

- Sci-Fi Dine-In Theater Restaurant

Hint 34: Face the kitchen, then look to the right of it at the tall fence. You'll find the classic Mickey you're seeking in the part of the mural that's above the right section of the fence. Look at the tree tops. The Hidden Mickey is part of the outline of the center-right top of a tree that is located to the right of a tall palm tree.

Hint 35: Watch the movie reel for Donald

Duck. He's in a cartoon segment about a secretary who is kidnapped to another planet. Donald is one of the characters who chases her.

- The Writer's Stop

Hint 36: Some of the theater lights hanging from the store ceiling sport yellow classic Mickeys.

- Toy Story Pizza Planet

Hint 37: A classic Mickey is one of the constellations of stars above the counter registers. Focus on the left side of the rear wall, between Woody and the "Disney's Toy Story" sign.

Hint 38: A small, bright classic-Mickey star appears above the counter registers on the right side of the rear wall. Look near the pizza-slice constellation.

Hint 39: Above the arcade games, in the moon near the top of the wall mural, you can spot a three-quarter Mickey profile facing left.

- Stage 1 Company Store

Hint 40: Look for an old bureau that's loaded with hats for sale and has paint cans at the very top. You'll find a green, painted classic Mickey near the center of the desktop.

Hint 41: Mickey Mouse's shorts (red with white buttons) are hanging on a line near one of the exit doors. (Thanks to my publisher Kelly Monaghan for admiring these designer shorts!)

- Mama Melrose's Ristorante Italiano

Hint 42: Just inside the entrance to the right, the Dalmatian has a black classic Mickey spot on its right shoulder (your left).

Hint 43: The right wall between the waiting room and the dining area bears a slightly distorted classic Mickey in the plas-

ter. It's in the upper right corner, near the entrance door.

Hint 44: To the right of the check-in podium (as you face it), a green classic Mickey leaf is about one and a half feet above the bottom of the window, along the left edge.

Hint 45: The left wall between the waiting room and the dining area has a smaller classic Mickey plastered on the brick. You'll find it in the middle left part of the wall, just above the counter.

- New York Street

Hint 46: A classic Mickey is in a window display at the end of New York Street near the Empire State Building. He's in the lower left part of a painting on the left wall. (Thanks to my sister Donna for spotting this artistic Hidden Mickey.)

- Intersection of Hollywood and Sunset Boulevards

Hint 47: On both sides of Sunset Boulevard near its intersection with Hollywood Boulevard, you'll find small impressions in the cement sidewalks, near the curb. They read, "Mortimer & Co, 1928 Contractors." Mortimer Mouse was Mickey Mouse's first (and soon discarded) name; 1928 was the year Mickey was "born."

- Keystone Clothiers

Hint 48: Outside and above the shop, a Kodak billboard shows a girl bending forward, partially covering Mickey Mouse's handprints impressed in cement.

- Mickey's of Hollywood

Hint 49: Classic Mickey holes are drilled in some of the metal support posts.

Hint 50: The caps on the ends of some

merchandise racks are shaped like classic Mickeys. (Thanks to John Perry, Jr. for showing this Hidden Mickey to me.)

Hint 51: In the Sorcerer section of the store, near a register and a door to the street, you'll find cabinets with classic Mickey shapes on them.

Hint 52: "MICKEY" is spelled out on four vertical dividers (two on each side of the store) that separate the sections of the store.

- Cover Story Store

Hint 53: You'll find a design containing classic Mickeys on the outside of the store, next to The Darkroom. Look below the second floor windows.

- Disney-MGM Studios Park Map

Hint 54: The face of Mickey Mouse on the upside-down park map has been distorted over time. The corners of his smile are still visible on both sides of the big Sorcerer's Hat, and his forehead "widow's peak" shows up just below where Hollywood Boulevard ends. (Look closely and you'll see that his smile and widow's peak are darker areas in the cement.) To the right, Echo Lake forms a distorted left ear.

- Fantasmic!

Hint 55: When animated characters float up in large bubbles on the water screen, watch for Pinocchio. His bubble forms the head of a classic Hidden Mickey. Two empty bubbles beside it form the ears.

★ Your first stop is **Kilimanjaro Safaris**. Walk through the Oasis, turn left in Discovery Island, and follow the path through Africa. Take the ride and look for a classic Hidden Mickey in the flamingo pond.

Clue 1: Observe the island in the pond.
4 points

★ Visit **DINOSAUR** next. Go back through Discovery Island and follow the walkway into DinoLand. Find a Hidden Mickey on a painting just inside the *DINOSAUR* building. (You can bypass the actual ride if you want.)

Clue 2: Can you spot the Hidden Mickey on a tree trunk?
4 points

Clue 3: Find a classic Mickey on the red dinosaur in the mural behind the counter in the ride's photo-purchase area.
4 points

★ Walk into the queue for **It's Tough to be a Bug!** on Discovery Island.

Clue 4: When you get inside *The Tree of Life*, look for a Hidden Mickey above the handicapped entrance doors.
4 points

★ Go to **Kali River Rapids** in Asia and find a classic Mickey formed by plates on the wall of one of the rooms you pass through on your way to the ride.

Clue 5: You're getting close when you see

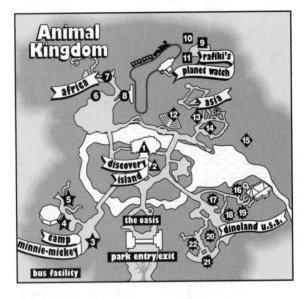

discovery island
1 The Tree of Life
2 It's Tough to be a Bug!

camp minnie-mickey
☆ Pocahontas and Her Forest Friends
☆ Festival of the Lion King
5 Character Greeting Trails

africa
6 Kilimanjaro Safaris
7 Pangani Forest Exploration Trail
8 Train to Rafiki's Planet Watch

rafiki's planet watch
9 Conservation Station
10 Affection Section
11 Habitat Habit!

asia
12 Flights of Wonder
13 Maharajah Jungle Trek
14 Kali River Rapids
15 Expedition EVEREST

dinoland u.s.a.
16 Tarzan™ Rocks! at Theater in the Wild
17 The Boneyard
18 TriceraTop Spin
19 Primeval Whirl
20 Cretaceous Trail
21 DINOSAUR
22 Dino-Sue T Rex

stone statues in the grass.
2 points

Clue 6: Further along in the queue, look for Hidden Mickeys above the entrance and exit doors (two above each door) of Mr. Paniki's Shop.
2 points to spot one or more

★ Stroll to the **Maharajah Jungle Trek**. At the tiger exhibit area, find six classic Hidden Mickeys in the building with arches.

Clue 7: Check swirls in the water to the right of the first arch.
2 points

Clue 8: Look for the earring Mickey on the left mural inside the first arch.
2 points

Clue 9: Find a leaf Mickey on the left mural inside the first arch.
2 points

Clue 10: Inside the building with arches, on the right wall, check the flowers on two square panels to find classic Mickeys.
2 points for one or more

Clue 11: Look for a classic Mickey in the mountains inside the second arch.
2 points

Clue 12: Now find a classic Mickey in the cloud formation inside the same arch.
2 points

Clue 13: Further along the trail, before you get to the aviary entrance, spot a classic Mickey in a man's necklace in the carving on the wall.
2 points

★ Before or after an early lunch, wander to the **Pangani Forest Exploration Trail** in Africa. Look for two classic HMs in the building with the Naked Mole Rat exhibit.

Clue 14: Study a small box of Asepso soap.
3 points

Clue 15: Spot a backpack with a Mickey emblem.
3 points

Clue 16: Past the gorilla viewing area, search for a Hidden Jafar.
5 points

★ Eat an early lunch to avoid the crowds. The Rainforest Café at the park entrance is a good place to eat and has an interesting ambiance. Tusker House Restaurant in Africa serves salads and sandwiches.

★ Consult the Times Guide and pick the next convenient show of **Pocahontas and Her Forest Friends** in Camp Minnie-Mickey.

Clue 17: In front of the theater entrance, try to find a birdhouse with a Mickey Mouse cutout.
1 point

(Periodically these birdhouses are moved around to different locations in Camp Minnie-Mickey; so it may not be here when you visit.)

Clue 18: Spot three rocks that form a classic Mickey on a dirt path near the stage.
3 points

Clue 19: After the show, find Mickey Mouse's head on top of a nearby **flagpole**.
4 points

★ Now search the camp for a **small cabin** with classic Mickeys in the woodwork.

Clue 20: You'll find them on both the front and sides of the cabin.
2 points for both

★ Go to Africa and take the *Wildlife Express Train* to Rafiki's Planet Watch for a

Hidden Mickey bonanza. In **Conservation Station** alone, you'll find 24 or more.

Clue 21: Find the Hidden Mickey profile in the changing, repeating panels inside the entrance.
5 points

Clue 22: On the wall mural just to the right, spot a Mickey Mouse profile on an opossum.
4 points

Clue 23: Look for a butterfly wearing classic Mickeys.
3 points

Clue 24: Gaze at a spider nearby with a classic Mickey marking.
3 points

Clue 25: Spot the classic Mickey on an ostrich.
3 points

Clue 26: Look for a classic Mickey on a green snake.
3 points

Clue 27: Locate a side profile Mickey Mouse on a hippopotamus.
4 points

Clue 28: Glance at a llama for a classic Mickey.
3 points

Clue 29: A squirrel nearby shows off a classic Mickey.
3 points

Clue 30: Spot a classic Mickey on an alligator.
3 points

Clue 31: Look for a frog with a tiny frontal face image of the Main Mouse.
5 points

Clue 32: Find the Hidden Mickey on an owl.
3 points

Clue 33: Search for the amazing Mickey image on a second butterfly!
5 points

Clue 34: Examine the grates around the bottoms of the trees in the main lobby.
2 points

Clue 35: Next to the "Song of the Rainforest" area, spot a fly with a tiny classic Mickey on its back.
5 points

Clue 36: Look for the classic Mickey shadow on the ceiling near door number eight in the "Song of the Rainforest" area.
4 points

Clue 37: Find a Hidden Mickey on a tree near door six in the "Song of the Rainforest" area.
3 points

Clue 38: Walk to the front of the Rainforest area and search for a side profile Mickey.
4 points

Clue 39: Look for a classic Mickey indentation on a tree toward the front of the Rainforest area.
3 points

Clue 40: Check the trees inside the Rainforest area for a side profile Mickey shadow.
4 points

Clue 41: Search for a green moss side profile Mickey in the Rainforest area.
4 points

Clue 42: Also in the "Song of the Rainforest" area, spot a classic Mickey on a cockroach.
4 points

Clue 43: Now find a classic Mickey on a lizard on the same tree.
3 points

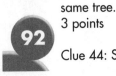

Clue 44: Spot a classic Mickey on a ledge

in the rear area displays and laboratories.
3 points

★ Walk outside to **Affection Section** to spot another classic Hidden Mickey.

Clue 45: Look closely at the fence on the stage.
2 points

★ Wander on over to the **Wildlife Express Train** station and look for classic Mickeys.

Clue 46: Examine the rafters inside the station.
2 points

★ Ride the train to Africa and explore the area around the **Harambe Fruit Market** to spot a large Mickey Mouse head in the cement.

Clue 47: Check the beginning of the cement and flagstone path at the side of the Fruit Market.
4 points

Clue 48: Turn left at the opposite end of the path and follow the cement walkway a few feet to find a large, faint classic Mickey in the cement.
5 points

★ Outside the **Mombasa Marketplace store**, look for a classic Mickey formed by a small utility cover and the pebbles adjacent to it.

Clue 49: It's near an entrance door to the store.
5 points

★ Walk to the far side of **Tamu Tamu Refreshments**.

Clue 50: Find another classic Mickey formed by a small utility cover and the pebbles adjacent to it.
5 points

Clue 51: Marvel at a Hidden Baloo inside the small seating area behind Tamu Tamu Refreshments.
5 points

★ Walk a short way down the **path to Asia**.

Clue 52: Look over to *The Tree of Life* and spot the Hidden Mickey on it. Psst! It's near the hippo.
4 points

★ Cross the bridge to Discovery Island and amble on into **Pizzafari restaurant** to find two Hidden Mickeys.

Clue 53: In the Nocturnal Room (the dining room directly to the left of the food counters as you face the counters), study the firefly wings.
3 points

Clue 54: In the large room past the Nocturnal Room, find some spots on the wall.
3 points

Clue 55: Outside Pizzafari restaurant, find Mickey on the side of a fire hydrant.
2 points

★ Return to DinoLand U.S.A. Enter **The Boneyard** and find three classic Mickeys.

Clue 56: Look under the drinking fountains inside the entrance.
3 points

Clue 57: Walk upstairs. Go to the rear and observe the small classic Mickey in an archeology display.
2 points

Clue 58: Look for Hidden Mickey hard hats in the children's dig area.
2 points

★ Walk to the **Cretaceous Trail** in the middle of DinoLand and go dino hunting.

Clue 59: Find a dark Hidden Mickey on a dinosaur's back.
3 points

★ Go to the parking spaces across from **TriceraTop Spin**.

Clue 60: Spot a classic Mickey in one of the spaces.
3 points

Clue 61: Study the nearby horned dinosaur studded with gems and find a Mickey pin.
4 points

★ Cross back to **Primeval Whirl** and look for classic Mickeys on the outside of the attraction.

Clue 62: Check the meteors.
3 points for one or more

Clue 63: Watch the parade (usually 4 p.m.) for classic Mickey headlights and a classic Mickey antenna.
3 points for both

★ Cross back to **Discovery Island** and find a classic Mickey made of green moss.

Clue 64: Study the front of *The Tree of Life*.
5 points

★ Keep your eyes open **as you leave the park**.

Clue 65: Outside the entrance turnstiles, check the metal grates around some of the trees near the tram loading area.
2 points

Total Points for Animal Kingdom =

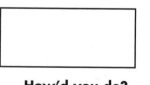

How'd you do?
Up to 83 points - Bronze
84 - 168 points - Silver
169 points and over - Gold
211 points - Perfect Score

**Caution:
Don't peek at this
section unless you
really want help!**

Africa

- *Kilimanjaro Safaris*

Hint 1: In elephant country, and about halfway through the ride, the island in the flamingo pond is shaped like a classic Hidden Mickey. It's to the left of the ride vehicle.

DinoLand U.S.A.

- *DINOSAUR*

Hint 2: Just inside the building entrance, on the right side of the queue, look at the tree at the far left of the painting. There's a classic Mickey on the tree trunk, across from a lower right branch.

Hint 3: On the mural behind the counter in the ride's photo-purchase area, a large red dinosaur has a small classic Mickey on its lower neck.

Discovery Island

- It's Tough to be a Bug!

Hint 4: Inside *The Tree of Life*, look for the handicapped entrance doors to *It's Tough to be a Bug!* (You reach them before you get to the main entrance doors to the theater.) Look at the upper left part of the green area above the doors to find a small classic Mickey.

Asia

- Kali River Rapids

Hint 5: Along the entrance queue, keep your eyes peeled for stone statues in the grass. As you enter the next room, look at the lower left corner of the wall. Three of the plates on the wall above the bicycle form a classic Mickey, tilted down to the right.

Hint 6: The design above the entrance and exit doors of Mr. Paniki's Shop includes small, gold classic Mickeys. You'll find two above each door.

- Maharajah Jungle Trek

Hint 7: To the right of the first arch, swirls in the water under a tiger form a classic Mickey.

Hint 8: Inside the first arch, on the left mural, the king's gold earring forms an upside-down classic Mickey.

Hint 9: Inside the first arch, on the left mural, three leaves under the wrist of the king's extended arm form a classic Mickey.

Hint 10: On the right wall inside the building with arches, two square panels are decorated with flowers. Some of the outer flowers have circles at the bases of their stems that form classic Mickeys.

Hint 11: Inside the second arch, on the left mural, there's a small classic Mickey in a brown rock formation on the left side of the mountains.

Hint 12: Inside the second arch, on the right mural, a classic Mickey appears in the upper part of the left cloud formation.

Hint 13: On a wall to the right, just before you reach the aviary entrance, you'll find an upside-down classic Mickey in the necklace of a man in the middle carving.

Africa

- Pangani Forest Exploration Trail

Hint 14: On the desk to the left of the entrance, a small box of Asepso soap behind the desk lamp has a classic Mickey as the "O" in Asepso.

Hint 15: In the far left corner of the room, a backpack sports a small classic Mickey emblem on the left side.

Hint 16: A three-dimensional head of Jafar is carved out of a rock 25 to 30 feet tall. It's past the gorilla viewing area, to the right of the first section of the first suspension bridge.

Camp Minnie-Mickey

- Pocahontas and Her Forest Friends

Hint 17: In front of the entrance to the theater, a birdhouse is often hanging from the front of Chip 'n' Dale's Cookie Cabin. It has a side profile cutout of Mickey Mouse.

Hint 18: On the lower part of the mural located just right of the stage, three rocks on a dirt path form a classic Mickey.

Hint 19: Mickey Mouse's head is on top of the flagpole by the water well opposite the entrance to *Pocahontas and Her Forest Friends* (and before you get to the second bridge to Camp Minnie-Mickey).

- cabin on the grounds

Hint 20: Across from the entrance to *Festival of the Lion King*, a small cabin housing an ice cream shop has classic Mickeys in the woodwork along the front and sides.

Rafiki's Planet Watch

- Conservation Station

Hint 21: The front wall inside the entrance has a section of changing, repeating panels. A small side profile of Mickey Mouse is in the center of the orange starfish.

Hint 22: Find an opossum on the right side of the mural just inside the entrance. There is a side profile of Mickey Mouse in its eye.

Hint 23: Above the opossum, at the upper right, you'll find a butterfly with classic Mickeys on its wings.

Hint 24: About six feet up from the floor, not far from the opossum, a spider has a light pink classic Mickey marking on its thorax. (Thanks to J. Baublitz for this and other HM sightings.)

Hint 25: On the wall to the left of the restrooms, near the entrance, the pupil of an ostrich's eye is a classic Mickey.

Hint 26: Toward the middle of the mural at the front, near the entrance, a green snake sports a black classic Mickey on its upper back.

Hint 27: A hippopotamus is the fifth animal from the left along the bottom of the entrance mural on the left wall. A side profile of Mickey Mouse is on its lower jaw, under the middle tooth.

Hint 28: To the immediate left of the hippopotamus, a llama sports a dark brown classic Mickey on its neck.

Hint 29: Under the hippopotamus, a squir-

rel has a black classic Mickey pupil.

Hint 30: On the right side of the hippopotamus, an alligator has a small dark classic Mickey to the left of its green eye.

Hint 31: To the right of the alligator, Mickey Mouse's face is under a frog's right eye.

Hint 32: A bit farther along on this left wall mural, the pupil of an owl's eye is a classic Mickey.

Hint 33: The entrance murals curve toward the inside of the building. Look for the butterfly with a full frontal image of Mickey Mouse on its body (not its wings!) on the right curving mural.

Hint 34: The grates around the bottoms of the trees in the main lobby of *Conservation Station* and outside by *Affection Section* have classic Mickey patterns.

Hint 35: The fly with a tiny classic Mickey on its back is on the left mural next to the "Song of the Rainforest" area.

Hint 36: Above and in front of door number eight in the "Song of the Rainforest" area, you can spot a dark classic Mickey shadow on the ceiling to the right.

Hint 37: A white classic Mickey is outlined on a tree by door six and to the left of the words "The Accidental Florist."

Hint 38: A side profile Mickey indentation appears on a tree under the "Song of the Rainforest" sign and to the lower right (as you face her) of Grandmother Willow's face.

Hint 39: Turn right just as you walk through the first entrance to the Rainforest area. The classic Mickey indentation is on a tree about four feet up from the floor.

Hint 40: A side profile Mickey shadow is

about seven feet up from the floor on the front of a tree inside the Rainforest area.

Hint 41: On the right side of the tree with "The Song of the Rainforest" sign, a rear horizontal panel has a green moss side profile Mickey about six feet up from the floor.

Hint 42: There is a cockroach display inside a tree in front of the "Song of the Rainforest" area. A cockroach inside and toward the back of the tree bears a dark classic Mickey on its back.

Hint 43: On that same tree, a lizard above the "Giant Cockroach" sign sports a classic Mickey.

Hint 44: A classic Mickey made of three containers with reptile skins is on a ledge in the far left window of a room with reptiles.

- Affection Section

Hint 45: On the stage by the animal petting area, blue dots near the middle of a fence form a classic Mickey.

- Wildlife Express Train

Hint 46: High up in the rafters inside the train station, look for classic Mickeys where the beams intersect.

Africa

- in and around Harambe

Hint 47: At one side of the Harambe Fruit Market, a short cement and flagstone path with benches leads through some trees. A large Mickey Mouse head in the cement marks the beginning of the path. It's several feet in diameter.

Hint 48: At the opposite end of this short path, turn left onto the cement walkway and walk a few feet. Nearby you'll find a faint depression in the cement that forms a very large classic Mickey (six feet or more in diameter). This HM is best seen after a rain when the pavement is wet.

Hint 49: Outside, near an entrance door to the Mombasa Marketplace store, you'll find a classic Mickey formed by a small utility cover (with the letter "D" in the middle) and the pebbles adjacent to it. The cover is on the the path on the side facing the Tusker House Restaurant.

Hint 50: Near Tamu Tamu Refreshments, on the walkway that connects Africa and Asia, a small utility cover and the pebbles adjacent to it form a similar classic Mickey. Here, the utility cover has the letter "S" in the middle.

Hint 51: Inside the small seating area behind Tamu Tamu Refreshments, a white Hidden Baloo is on the wall nearest the path to Asia. He's often covered by a curtain.

Hint 52: On the back of *The Tree of Life*, and visible from the path between Africa and Asia, is an upside-down classic Mickey above the eye of the hippopotamus.

Discovery Island

- *Pizzafari restaurant*

Hint 53: On the left rear wall of the Nocturnal Room (the dining room directly to the left of the food counters as you face the counters), the wings of the lower left firefly resemble Mickey Mouse ears.

Hint 54: On the far wall in the room past the Nocturnal Room, a gray spot with two white ears forms a classic Mickey in the tree branches to the right of the leopard.

Hint 55: The fire hydrant with the classic Mickey on its side sits across from Pizzafari restaurant, in front of the Island Mercantile shop. Take a good look at Mickey's ears; they're multicolored circles.

DinoLand U.S.A.

- The Boneyard

Hint 56: Just inside the entrance, you'll find a reddish-brown classic Mickey pattern in the flooring under the drinking fountains.

Hint 57: Upstairs to the rear left, in a fenced off archeology display, three coins on a table form a classic Mickey.

Hint 58: On the right side of the children's dig area, in a small display, a fan and two hard hats form a classic Mickey.

- Cretaceous Trail

Hint 59: At one end of this short trail in the middle of DinoLand, you'll find a large dinosaur. Three dark spots on its middle back form a classic Mickey.

- TriceraTop Spin

Hint 60: In the parking spaces across from *TriceraTop Spin*, a classic Mickey can be found in the cement at the front of the second parking space from the horned dinosaur.

Hint 61: On the right side of the horned dinosaur (as you face it), a gold "Steamboat Willie" cast member pin is located toward the rear, near a large silver medallion.

- Primeval Whirl

Hint 62: In the outside decorations, the sides of several meteors sport classic Mickey craters.

Hint 63: The parade (usually at 4 p.m.) abounds in classic and décor Mickeys. The first jeep has classic Mickey headlights and the last vehicle has classic Mickey antenna dishes on the flagpole. (Thanks to F. van Wijk for these sightings.)

104

Discovery Island

- The Tree of Life

Hint 64: On the front of *The Tree of Life*, facing the Oasis and about one-third the distance up the trunk from the bottom, is a classic Mickey made of green moss. You'll find it to the left of the buffalo.

Outside the entrance turnstiles to the park

Hint 65: Outside the entrance turnstiles, near the tram loading area, the metal grates at the base of some of the trees incorporate classic Mickeys in their design.

CHAPTER 6

Resort Hotel Scavenger Hunt

••••••••••••••••••••••••••••••••

Walt Disney World's resort hotels are filled with Mickeys, hidden and otherwise. The majority are what I like to call décor Hidden Mickeys, imaginative decorations that vary among the hotels and change periodically over time. Such Hidden Mickeys can be found along hotel hallways in the carpet, wallpaper, and lampshades. They appear in the guest rooms on covers for drinking glasses, bedspreads, pillows, day beds, furniture, lamps, lampshades, room curtains, shower curtains, wall pictures, wallpaper, carpets, soap, the outer wrapping of toilet paper rolls, and other items. Guest laundry rooms sometimes have Hidden Mickeys on the soap vending machines and in the bubbles on wall paintings. In the restaurants, pancakes, waffles, butter pats, pasta, pizza, pepperoni on the pizza, and the arrangement of dishes and condiments, among other items, are sometimes Mickey-shaped. And Mickey Mouse imprints can often be found in the sand in hotel ashtrays.

Mugs, paper plates, and other items in the gift shops can sport hiding Mickeys. Even the utilities embrace Mickey. Manhole covers and survey markers throughout Walt Disney World often have classic Mickey designs in the center.

Generally, I do not include such décor Mickeys in the scavenger hunts unless they are truly unique and are easily accessible to Hidden Mickey hunters at the hotels and other WDW areas. So don't be surprised to discover dozens of Mickeys at the hotels you visit that aren't included in this scavenger hunt. They're fun to spot but you don't get points for finding them.

The best way to hunt for Hidden Mickeys at the hotels is by car. Buses to all the WDW hotels are available from Downtown Disney (the major bus depot is at the far end of the Mar-

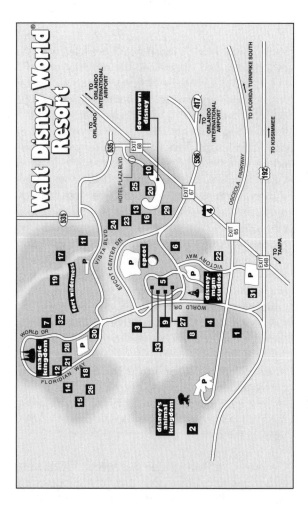

1 All-Star Resorts
2 Animal Kingdom Lodge
3 Beach Club
4 Blizzard Beach
5 BoardWalk
6 Caribbean Beach
7 Contemporary
8 Coronado Springs
9 Dolphin
10 Downtown Disney
11 Eagle Pines Golf Course
12 Grand Floridian
13 Lake Buena Vista Golf Course
14 Magnolia Golf Course
15 Oak Trails Golf Course
16 Old Key West
17 Osprey Ridge Golf Course
18 Palm Golf Course

19 Pioneer Hall
20 Pleasure Island, in Downtown Disney
21 Polynesian
22 Pop Century
23 Port Orleans French Quarter
24 Port Orleans Riverside
25 Saratoga Springs
26 Shades of Green
27 Swan
28 Transportation and Ticket Center
29 Typhoon Lagoon
30 WDW Speedway
31 Wide World of Sports
32 Wilderness Lodge
33 Yacht Club
P Parking

ketplace). If you choose to bus around, be prepared for leisurely hunting. You won't be able to visit as many hotels in a given time frame as you would with a car.

Of course, driving means parking, and it's not always a slam-dunk. Guard gates stand watch at most WDW hotels. When you drive up, tell the guard that you're a Hidden Mickey freak and want to look for Hidden Mickeys at the hotel. You'll generally be greeted with a smile, an opened gate, and a wave—along with a "Good luck!" or "Go freak out!" to encourage you on your quest. In the event you aren't allowed to park, drive on to another hotel on the scavenger hunt and take transportation (bus, boat or monorail) to the one you want to explore. If you're really lucky, you may have a spouse, friend or family member who is willing to drop you off and pick you up.

Again, be considerate of other guests and cast members. Ask permission to look around restaurants and avoid searching for Hidden Mickeys at meal times unless you are one of the diners. Even then be careful to stay out of the way—especially of waiters with full trays. Let others share in the fun by telling them what you are up to if they notice you looking around.

Two important notes:
• I've arranged this hunt in a logical, efficient progression that I imagine you could follow in a car. However, you may want to hunt just one hotel or group of sister hotels at a time. That's why I list the perfect score for each resort hotel (and hotel group) in parentheses after the hotel (or group) name in the Clues section.

• This scavenger hunt includes only those WDW resorts in which I found Hidden Mickeys. If I found no convincing (to me) Hidden Mickeys in a hotel, I didn't include it in the hunt. Keep your eyes open; you may spot a Hidden Mickey that I haven't found (yet).

I'll start with the Animal Kingdom Lodge Resort, but you can start (and stop) wherever you want.

 **110** Have fun!

Animal Kingdom Lodge Resort
(61 points)

Clue 1: Look up for a classic Mickey outside near the hotel's main entrance.
2 points

Clue 2: Find a classic Mickey on a wall mural between the outer and inner entrance doors to the main lobby.
2 points

Clue 3: Inside the main lobby, spot a classic Mickey on a chandelier.
3 points

Clue 4: Check the logs banded to wood supports around the main lobby. Find any classic Mickeys?
2 points

Clue 5: Look for a classic Mickey on the rock formation next to the short bridge on the right side of the main lobby (as you face it on entering).
4 points

Clue 6: Try to spot a green Hidden Mickey in side profile outside the rear doors of the main lobby. He's on the vine-covered column, on your right as you exit, and he's looking into the lobby.
5 points

Clue 7: On the trail to Arusha Rock Overlook, outside the rear exit from the main lobby, explore the decorative reliefs on the rock wall for a giraffe with a classic Mickey.
3 points

Clue 8: Spot another classic Mickey along the walkway in Arusha Rock Overlook.
4 points

Clue 9: Search for a classic Mickey on the rock wall as you descend the stairs from the right side of the main lobby to Boma restaurant.
4 points

Clue 10: Examine the chairs inside Boma restaurant.
2 points

Clue 11: Inside Jiko restaurant, check out the ceiling above the large oven exhausts.
2 points

Clue 12: From the path alongside the walkway to the pool's water slide, find a classic Mickey impression low on a rock.
4 points

Clue 13: Further along this walkway, around the back of the swimming pool, look for a light-colored classic Mickey cut into the rock wall.
3 points

Clue 14: From a fence at the flamingo overlook, study the rock wall for a classic Mickey.
4 points

Clue 15: Search the wall outside in the back of The Mara eatery seating area for a classic Mickey.
4 points

Now find three classic Mickeys inside The Mara food area.

Clue 16: One is on the left upper wall.
3 points

Clue 17: Another is above the bakery.
3 points

Clue 18: The third is on the right upper wall.
3 points

Clue 19: Spot a classic Mickey in the elevator to the Fitness Center.
2 points

Clue 20: Walk around to spot some classic Mickeys in the carpet.
2 points for one or more

Disney's All-Star Resorts
(10 points)

★ *All-Star Sports Resort* (4 points)

Clue 21: Go to the main building gift shop and find classic Mickeys in the carpet.
2 points

Clue 22: Find the classic Mickey in the cement outdoors behind and to the right of the registration building. Psst! He's near the Mickey Mouse statue.
2 points

★ *All-Star Music Resort* (5 points)

Clue 23: Examine the Jazz Inn courtyard to spot classic Mickey ears.
3 points

Clue 24: Take a look at the boots in the Country Fair area.
2 points

★ *All-Star Movies Resort* (1 point)

Clue 25: Check out Andy's Room in the resort's "Toy Story" section.
1 point

Coronado Springs Resort
(18 points)

Clue 26: Take a good look at the large wooden doors at the front entrance to the main lobby.
3 points

Clue 27: Observe the interior design in Francisco's Lounge.
2 points

Clue 28: Examine the cement near the Marina rental gazebo.
4 points

Clue 29: Find a classic Mickey on a wall at the Dig Site swimming pool.
3 points

Clue 30: Now look for a whitish classic Mickey on a stone block on the Mayan pyramid at the Dig Site.
4 points

Clue 31: Check the bus stop signs around the periphery of the resort.
2 points for one or more

Pop Century Resort
(5 points)

Clue 32: Look low for Hidden Mickeys at the Everything Pop food court.
3 points for two or more

Clue 33: In the shop adjoining the Everything Pop food court, find Hidden Mickeys on merchandise stands.
2 points

Caribbean Beach Resort
(2 points)

Clue 34: Spot a classic Mickey on the lighthouse behind Old Port Royale.
2 points

Downtown Disney Area Resorts
(33 points)

★ *Old Key West Resort* (16 points)

Clue 35: Check out the fences in Conch Flats General Store.
2 points

Clue 36: Take a close look at the fence railings in the registration area.
2 points

Clue 37: Notice these same railings on the guest buildings outside.
2 points

★ Search for classic Mickeys formed by three shell imprints in the cement on the paths leading from parking spaces to Building 36.

Clue 38: Search the cement on the right side of the first path for imprints.
5 points

Clue 39: On the second path, explore the corner of the sidewalk after the first right turn.
5 points

(More of these amazing Mickeys may be scattered around the resort.)

★ *Port Orleans Resort - French Quarter* (2 points)

Clue 40: Look up for a classic Mickey in the food court area.
2 points

★ *Port Orleans Resort - Riverside* (9 points)

Clue 41: Look for classic Mickeys in the latticework of the registration area.
2 points

Clue 42: Also in the registration area, find more classic Mickeys near the giant fans.
2 points

Clue 43: Take a good look at the Native American statue in Colonel's Cotton Mill Food Court.
3 points

Clue 44: Check the outside railings on the resort's guest buildings.
2 points

★ *Saratoga Springs Resort* (6 points)

Clue 45: Notice classic Mickeys near The Turf Club.
2 points

Clue 46: Find more Mickey images inside.
2 points for one or more

Clue 47: Admire the guest buildings.
2 points

Epcot Resorts
(41 points)

To explore the following hotels, park at one and walk to the others around Crescent Lake. Smile and tell the guards that you're searching for Hidden Mickeys.

★ *BoardWalk Resort* (12 points)

Clue 48: Spot two classic Mickeys on a horse in the main lobby.
3 points

Clue 49: Find classic Mickeys on lamps in the center of the lobby.
2 points for one or more

Clue 50: Wander around the guest room and elevator hallways.
3 points for finding Mickeys in two sizes

Clue 51: Examine the trays above the cooking area in Spoodles restaurant.
2 points

Clue 52: Check the crockery on the shelves above the counters in the BoardWalk Bakery.
2 points

★ *Beach Club Resort* (20 points)

Clue 53: Search for Mickey Mouse along the inside walkway in front of the Cape May Café.
3 points

Walk to the Beach Club Solarium to find more Hidden Mickeys. Psst! Check the walls.

Clue 54: Spot some car tires with Mickey's face (frontal full view).
3 points

Clue 55: Now look for classic Mickeys in the same general area.
2 points

Clue 56: Gaze at Mickey's face in the sky.
3 points

Clue 57: Then find classic Mickeys in the water.
2 points

Clue 58: Do you see another classic Mickey floating in the air?
2 points

Clue 59: Walk to a guest room hallway to find classic Mickeys.
2 points for one or more

Clue 60: Look down into the Beach Club main lobby for two classic Mickeys.
3 points for spotting both

★ *Yacht Club Resort* (9 points)

Clue 61: Look for the corner table in the main lobby with character names on the drawers.
4 points

Clue 62: In the Yachtsman Steakhouse, find the photograph of (now deceased) Minnie Moo, a cow born with a black classic Mickey on her side. (You may have to ask a cast member where the photo is located. It's sometimes not on public display.)
5 points

Wilderness Lodge Resort
(67 points)

Clue 63: Check out the signs on the right side of the entrance drive.
2 points

Clue 64: Spot a classic Mickey on the guard gate kiosk.
2 points

Clue 65: Look up for a classic Mickey etched in a support pole in the car unloading area.
4 points

Clue 66: Look hard for a classic Mickey etched in another support pole and partially hidden under a black metal band.
4 points

Clue 67: Glance down for a tiny classic Mickey traced in the cement on a black stripe.
5 points

Clue 68: Look up again for a classic Mickey etched on a side support pole.
4 points

Clue 69: Find a classic Mickey on a large key in the registration area.
1 point

Clue 70: Look for Mickey driving a bus overhead.
2 points

Clue 71: Find a classic Mickey on the rock of the main lobby fireplace.
5 points

Clue 72: Peek at a fireplace inside the Whispering Canyon Cafe for a classic Mickey. (Ask a cast member to let you into the rear of the cafe.)
3 points

Clue 73: Look for a classic Mickey on a wall map at the entrance stairs to the Territory Lounge.
3 points

Clue 74: Now go inside and spot a classic Mickey on a ceiling mural above the bar.
4 points

Clue 75: Inside the Artist Point restaurant, spot a classic Mickey in a large mural above the entrance to the rear left dining area. Psst! The Mickey is hiding in a tree.
3 points

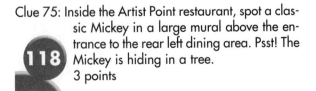

Clue 76: Locate a classic Mickey near Room 6100.
3 points

Clue 77: Explore one floor down for a classic Mickey near Room 5066.
3 points

Clue 78: Find another classic Mickey near Room 4035.
3 points

Clue 79: Search for a classic Mickey in the rock outside at Fire Rock Geyser.
4 points

Clue 80: Find stairs outside an exit door from the main building (on the side toward the Boat and Bike Rental) and look up for a classic Mickey.
4 points

- in the Cubs Den

(Tip: Visit in the afternoon if possible. It's less crowded then, and the cast members are more likely to let you in. Tell them you're searching for Hidden Mickeys.)

Clue 81: Spot a plush Mickey doll in a mural.
2 points

Clue 82: Look higher for a side profile Mickey.
3 points

Clue 83: Find a classic Mickey in the same mural.
3 points

Magic Kingdom Monorail Resorts
(39 points)

To find the Hidden Mickeys in these resorts and the nearby Wedding Pavilion, park at the Polynesian or the Grand Floridian and ride the monorail to the other two resorts and past the Wedding Pavilion. Or if you prefer, you can walk or drive to the Wedding Pavilion.

Note: The Polynesian has the bigger parking lot.

★ *Polynesian Resort* (16 points)

Clue 84: On the lower level, look for a classic Mickey on the floor near the waterfall.
3 points

Clue 85: Study the bamboo ring wall decorations by the corner staircase.
3 points

Find two Hidden Mickeys in Trader Jack's gift shop.

Clue 86: Look on top of the merchandise cabinets in front of the upper wall mural.
1 point

Clue 87: Now check out the chair.
2 points

Clue 88: At the Kona Island Coffee Bar, search for a small classic Mickey on top of the counter.
5 points

Clue 89: Observe the sign for Moana Mickey's Arcade outside the main building.
2 points

★ *Wedding Pavilion* (3 points)

(Note: A Hidden Mickey may be lurking inside the main building, but the building isn't open to the general public.)

Clue 90: As your monorail car passes by the pavilion buildings, observe the weather vane.
3 points

★ *Grand Floridian Resort* (6 points)

The Hidden Mickeys here are all classic Mickeys.

Clue 91: Take a good look at the weather vanes on the roofs.
3 points for one or more

Clue 92: Check out the large trolley carts outside the hotel.
1 point

Clue 93: Find some Hidden Mickeys in the hallways.
2 points for one or more

★ *Contemporary Resort* (14 points)

Clue 94: From the window of the California Grill restaurant, on the top floor, spot a stretched out Mickey watchband on the ground in front of the hotel.
4 points

Clue 95: Check out the (closed) glass doors of the back room inside the California Grill restaurant. (If the doors are open, you may not see the Hidden Mickey.)
3 points

Clue 96: Go to the sixth floor and walk in the direction of the Transportation and Ticket Center to an outside balcony to spot this amazing Hidden Mickey.
5 points

Clue 97: Find a classic Mickey silhouette in the bricks behind the main hotel. Psst! It's near Mickey Mouse himself.
2 points

Now tally up your scores while enjoying a treat from the food court inside the hotel.

Total Points for Hotel Hunt =

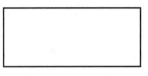

How'd you do?

A perfect score for this scavenger hunt is 276. But here is a breakdown by resort and resort group, so that you compare your score with the perfect score for the areas you've covered. You'll find the total points for each section in parentheses. Give yourself gold if you score at least 80% of the points available.

Animal Kingdom Lodge Resort (61)

Disney's All-Star Resorts (10)
   All-Star Sports Resort (4)
   All-Star Music Resort (5)
   All-Star Movies Resort (1)

Coronado Springs Resort (18)

Pop Century Resort (5)

Caribbean Beach Resort (2)

Downtown Disney Area Resorts (33)
   Old Key West Resort (16)
   Port Orleans French Quarter Resort (2)
   Port Orleans Riverside Resort (9)
   Saratoga Springs Resort (6)

Epcot Resorts (41)
   BoardWalk Resort (12)
   Beach Club Resort (20)
   Yacht Club Resort (9)

Wilderness Lodge Resort (67)

Magic Kingdom Monorail Resorts (39)
   Polynesian Resort (16)
   Wedding Pavilion (3)
   Grand Floridian Resort (6)
   Contemporary Resort (14)

**Caution:
Don't peek at this
section unless you
really want help!**

Animal Kingdom Lodge Resort

Hint 1: Outside, above the lower roof, the second tall figure to the left of the car baggage drop-off area has a classic Mickey in his mouth.

Hint 2: On the right wall mural between the outer and inner entrance doors to the main lobby, an orange and brown creature sports a classic Mickey in a circle on its mid back.

Hint 3: Inside the main lobby, you can find a classic Mickey near the bottom of the second chandelier on the right (as you face in from the front entrance). The Hidden Mickey is near the bottom of one of the shields.

Hint 4: Around the main lobby, classic Mickeys are formed by logs banded to wood supports. One of the best is the second support on the right (as you enter the lobby from the front doors). It's on the second level, on the side away from the main lobby entrance.

Hint 5: On the right side of the main lobby (as you face in from the front entrance), a short bridge crosses a rockbound pool of water. A classic Mickey is visible on the rock from the side of the bridge nearest the lobby. It's toward the rear on the right side. To spot it, look for the first recess in the rock from the right edge of the pool. Mickey is at the back of this recess, above the water line.

Hint 6: Outside the rear doors from the main lobby, a green Mickey in side profile hides in the decorative vines to the right as you exit. He is about two-thirds of the way up the side of the vine-covered column, above the middle horizontal brace. Look for him at the top of an open space in the vines. He's looking into the lobby.

Hint 7: Outside the rear exit from the main lobby, on the left side of the trail to Arusha Rock Overlook, check the rock wall for a decorative relief of a group of giraffes. You'll find a classic Mickey among the spots on the middle of the large giraffe in the center.

Hint 8: Along the walkway in Arusha Rock Overlook, a rock sports a classic Mickey. Look for it where the trail first turns left between rock walls. It's on the right side in the first small alcove, about six feet up from the path and under a large overhanging rock.

Hint 9: Toward the bottom of the staircase that winds from the right side of the main lobby to Boma restaurant, there's a classic Mickey on the rock wall next to a waterfall.

Hint 10: Inside Boma restaurant, you'll see classic Mickeys on some of the chairs with tall metal backs.

Hint 11: Inside Jiko restaurant, a classic Mickey is formed on the ceiling above the two large orange oven exhausts and the white column behind them.

Hint 12: Outside the exit from the restaurants, a large rock on the left side of the path behind the water slide has a classic Mickey impressed on its lower half near the ground. The rock is about three-quarters of the way along the walkway to the water slide. A small light pole juts out of the top of this rock.

Hint 13: A light-colored classic Mickey is cut into a rock wall behind the swimming pool. The wall forms the back of the pool's water slide. The Mickey is several feet above the walkway, below a gazebo that marks the starting point for the water slide.

Hint 14: Walk behind the pool to the bird and flamingo overlook. From the rightmost Bird Spotter Guide on the fence along the main trail, look to your right to the opposite fence. About two-thirds of the distance along this fence from the main trail, a pinkish classic Mickey with a white right ear is about one foot down from the top of the rock.

Hint 15: A classic stone Mickey is on the rear of the short wall behind The Mara seating area. It's about three feet up from the ground, behind an emergency phone and a tall brown pole.

HInt 16: In the food area of The Mara, a classic Mickey is on the upper left wall in the third leaf from the left tree (in the mural of falling leaves).

Hint 17: A tiny green classic Mickey is on the mural with green foliage above the bakery. He's hiding just above the bottom rim and facing the wine cabinet.

Hint 18: A classic Mickey is in a leaf in the middle of the upper right mural of falling leaves in the food area.

Hint 19: As you enter the elevator to the Fitness Center, you can spot a classic Mickey on the lower left panel (as you face the rear of the elevator).

Hint 20: Many red classic Mickeys can be found in the carpet in the hallways in front of guest rooms.

Disney's All-Star Resorts

- All-Star Sports Resort

Hint 21: In the main building gift shop, classic Mickeys are part of the carpet. Each is composed of a baseball with two circles for ears.

Hint 22: Outside, behind and to the right of the registration building, a large Mickey Mouse statue stands directly over a classic Mickey (white head and black ears) in the cement.

- All-Star Music Resort

Hint 23: In the Jazz Inn courtyard, classic Mickey ears top the cymbal stands. Each is a winged nut that holds a cymbal in place. (These nuts come and go.)

Hint 24: In the Country Fair area, you'll find classic Mickeys on the fronts and backs of the huge boots.

- All-Star Movies Resort

Hint 25: The large checkers in Andy's Room in the "Toy Story" section sport classic Mickeys.

Coronado Springs Resort

Hint 26: Some of the medallions on the large, open wooden doors at the front entrance to the main lobby are three-dimensional reliefs of Mickey's face.

Hint 27: Mickey ears are part of the design over the bar at Francisco's Lounge, inside the main building.

Hint 28: A classic Mickey is chipped into the cement by the lamppost nearest the Marina rental gazebo.

Hint 29: At the Dig Site swimming pool's main entrance (closest to the lake), a classic Mickey hides on a wall to your left as you enter. It's at the upper left of the wall

facing the pool.

Hint 30: Also at the Dig Site, you'll find a whitish classic Mickey near the very top of the Mayan pyramid, on the side facing the pool. It's on the second stone block from the left, a few rows from the top.

Hint 31: Mickey Mouse (side profile) is sitting in a bus on some of the bus stop signs (such as at Bus Stop #4) located around the periphery of the resort.

Pop Century Resort

Hint 32: Several classic Mickeys are hiding on the tile floor of the food court order area. One is near the merchandise stand in the center of the order and pay area. Another is in front of the middle cash register.

Hint 33: In the shop near the food court, classic Mickey holes are in the poles that hold merchandise racks.

Caribbean Beach Resort

Hint 34: Behind Old Port Royale, a classic Mickey appears in the "Barefoot Bay Boat Yard" sign on the side of the lighthouse near the bike racks.

Downtown Disney Area Resorts

- Old Key West Resort

Hint 35: The design in the fence woodwork throughout Conch Flats General Store includes classic Mickeys.

Hint 36: Classic Mickeys are worked into the design of the fence railings behind the check-in counter in the registration area.

Hint 37: You'll see these same railings outside, around the floors of the guest buildings.

Hints 38 and 39: Classic Mickeys formed by three shell imprints in the cement can be found on the two paths leading from parking spaces to Building 36. On the first path, you'll find the Hidden Mickey just after the first right turn on the right side. On the second path, the three shell imprints are in the corner of the sidewalk, after the first right turn and just before the next left turn.

- Port Orleans Resort - French Quarter

Hint 40: Upside-down classic Mickeys made of blue and white gemstones adorn the top of a crown hanging from the ceiling on the right side of the food court seating area.

- Port Orleans Resort - Riverside

Hint 41: Above the registration area, classic Mickeys are repeated in the wooden latticework circling the central lobby.

Hint 42: In the registration area, classic Mickeys decorate the sides of the brackets holding the giant fans hanging from the ceiling above the center of the lobby.

Hint 43: In Colonel's Cotton Mill Food Court, you will find black classic Mickeys on the moccasins of a Native American statue near the bakery.

Hint 44: The outside railings around the floors of the guest buildings contain classic Mickeys.

- Saratoga Springs Resort

Hint 45: In the hallway leading to The Turf Club, the jacket in the second display on the left sports black classic Mickeys.

Hint 46: On a left side wall inside The Turf Club, Mickey and other characters decorate billiard balls in the first display to the left.

Hint 47: Some balcony railings on the guest buildings have classic Mickey holes.

Epcot Resorts

- BoardWalk Resort

Hint 48: In the main lobby, an outside horse on the small carousel has brown spots that form two classic Mickeys.

Hint 49: Classic Mickeys hold the shades in place on the lamps facing the fireplace in the center of the lobby.

Hint 50: Large classic Mickeys hide in the carpet in front of some elevators, while smaller ones appear in the guest room hallway carpets.

Hint 51: In Spoodles restaurant, three brass trays high above the cooking area are arranged to form a classic Mickey.

Hint 52: In the BoardWalk Bakery, a black and white Mickey Mouse sugar bowl is on the left upper shelf, above the counters. He's sitting by Pinocchio.

- Beach Club Resort

Hint 53: Along the inside walkway in front of the Cape May Café, a full length Mickey Mouse is standing in a sandcastle. It's the sculpture farthest to the left, on the wall facing the pool.

Hint 54: Enter the Solarium from the Beach Club main lobby. The first painting on the wall to your left has Mickey's face on spare tires on the backs of the yellow car (left side) and the blue car (right side).

Hint 55: Classic Mickey hood ornaments adorn the blue and red cars on the right of this painting.

Hint 56: In the second painting on the left wall, you can see Mickey's face looking out at you from the clouds at the upper right.

129

Hint 57: The cruise ship smokestacks in this second painting have classic Mickey decals.

Hint 58: A Mickey balloon is on the right side of the third painting to your left.

Hint 59: The guest room hallways have carpet segments with classic Mickeys, some inside seashells.

Hint 60: Some of the bubbles (only a few!) in the large rugs covering the Beach Club main lobby form classic Mickeys. A strange purple classic Mickey (disguised as a sea urchin?) also floats around in them.

- Yacht Club Resort

Hint 61: In a seating area in the main lobby, the names of Mickey, Minnie, Donald, Daisy, Goofy, and Huey are on small labels on the drawers of a corner cabinet. (This cabinet is moved around at times to different parts of the lobby.)

Hint 62: A photograph of (now deceased) Minnie Moo, a cow born with a black classic Mickey on her side, often hangs in the Yachtsman Steakhouse near the end of the entrance walkway. It's on a right hand wall, past the podium. Minnie Moo once resided at Fort Wilderness.

Wilderness Lodge Resort

Hint 63: On the right side of the entrance drive to the hotel, a full length Mickey Mouse is walking on top of the "Bear Crossing" sign.

Hint 64: A classic Mickey is on the slanted end of the first horizontal log beam of the guard gate kiosk as your car approaches the entrance gate.

Hint 65: As you approach the center steps from the parking lot, you'll see that the roof of the covered unloading area in front of the entrance is supported by

huge wooden logs, banded together (four to a set) by black metal strips. The right rear pole of the first set to the right (as you face the entrance) has a classic Mickey etched in the wood above the upper black metal band. This Mickey faces the parking lot.

Hint 66: In the set of support poles on the left after you walk up the center steps from the parking lot, the pole in the corner closest to you and the entrance to the hotel has a classic Mickey etched in the wood. This Mickey is partially covered by the upper black metal band; only his head and part of his right ear are visible. This Mickey faces the steps.

Hint 67: In the cement of the car drive-through, the black stripe nearest the center steps from the parking lot has a tiny classic Mickey. From the red rectangle in the cement, follow the right (as you face the hotel entrance) diagonal crack to the black stripe. The tiny classic Mickey is traced in the cement about six inches to the right of the intersection of the crack and the stripe.

Hint 68: As you face the hotel entrance, the left rear support pole of the far left set of poles closest to the parking lot has a classic Mickey etched in the wood. It's above the lateral crossbeam on the lower part of the pole.

Hint 69: A classic Mickey hides on the left side of a large key in a wall display behind the registration counter. Look near the entrance to the Mercantile Shop.

Hint 70: A sign that says, "Walt Disney World Transportation," hangs from the ceiling near the Mercantile Shop. Mickey (in side profile) is driving the bus at the top of it.

Hint 71: In the lobby, you'll find a classic Mickey on the rock in the corner to the upper right of the fireplace. Search at the level of the lower round wooden horizontal beam that juts toward the lobby.

Hint 72: At a fireplace in the rear room of the Whispering Canyon Cafe, bend down low and look for a classic Mickey cut out of the outer grillwork. It is the third icon from the left corner along the bottom row of icons.

Hint 73: At the entrance stairs to the Territory Lounge, a classic Mickey decorates a pot in the right lower section of a wall map.

Hint 74: Inside the Territory Lounge, you'll find a classic Mickey on the rear of a beige mule in a ceiling mural. Look above the center of the bar.

Hint 75: Inside the Artist Point restaurant, examine the large mural above the entrance to the rear left dining area. You can spot a classic Mickey in the upper part of the lowest tree on the right if you look between the third and fourth lights (counting from the left) illuminating the mural.

Hint 76: A classic Mickey is etched near the bottom of a flat vertical wooden post around the corner from Room 6100 and near a green EXIT sign.

Hint 77: Near room 5066, a classic Mickey is etched on a flat, wooden vertical post about five and a half feet from the floor. It's across from an ice machine.

Hint 78: A classic Mickey is etched on a vertical wooden post about six feet up from the floor across from Room 4035. (Thanks to J. Bridge for this HM.)

Hint 79: Outside, from the walkway next to Fire Rock Geyser, scan the shallow stream running down from the small pool by the geyser. A classic Mickey is in the rock of the streambed about a third of the way up to the geyser.

Hint 80: Walk toward the Boat and Bike Rental and locate stairs at an exit door in the corner of the main building. A classic Mickey is indented in a vertical wooden beam at the left side of the exit door (as you face the door) across from the fourth floor balcony. Mickey is on the right side of the beam. (Thanks to J. Bridge for this one, too.)

- in the Cub's Den

Hint 81: A plush Mickey doll sits in the rightmost teepee in the mural on the right wall.

Hint 82: In this same mural, a side profile shadow of Mickey (standing and looking right) falls on the side of a mountain to the right of center of the mural and above the tree line.

Hint 83: On the far left of this mural, midway up and left of the mountains, is a classic Mickey.

Magic Kingdom Monorail Resorts

- Polynesian Resort

Hint 84: On the lower level, just inside the main lobby, there's a classic Mickey design in the flagstone tiles a few feet in front of the waterfall.

Hint 85: Along the corner staircase from the lobby, wall decorations have bamboo rings. Seen end on, some of the lower rings in the right side decoration form classic Mickeys.

Hint 86: In Trader Jack's gift shop, Mickey Mouse is sitting in a chair on top of some merchandise cabinets. He's in front of the upper wall mural.

Hint 87: You'll find classic Mickeys on the arms of that chair.

Hint 88: At the Kona Island Coffee Bar, in front of the Kona Café, small purple tiles on top of the mosaic tile counter form a classic Mickey. You'll spot it to the left of the glass case.

Hint 89: Outside the main building, the sign for Moana Mickey's Arcade has a classic Mickey on the top end of Mickey's spear.

- Wedding Pavilion

Hint 90: The weather vane on top of the building closest to the monorail has a full-length side profile of Mickey Mouse.

- Grand Floridian Resort

Hint 91: Weather vanes on various roofs at the front of the resort sport classic Mickeys.

Hint 92: The large trolley carts outside the hotel have classic Mickeys in the woodwork around the luggage storage areas at the back of the carts.

Hint 93: Most guest room hallways have classic Hidden Mickeys in the wallpaper.

- Contemporary Resort

Hint 94: From the window of the California Grill restaurant on the top floor, you can see a stretched out Mickey watchband on the ground in front of the hotel. It's among the conical-shaped trees. (You can see part of this watchband from the monorail.)

Hint 95: Inside the California Grill restaurant, a classic Mickey is frosted in the design of the (closed) glass doors of the back room.

Hint 96: From a sixth floor outside balcony closest to the front of the hotel, look left to see Mickey sitting on the edge of a roof below! This Mickey can also be spotted from either monorail.

Hint 97: Behind the main hotel, a classic Mickey silhouette can be found in the bricks under the metal Mickey Mouse sculpture. (The sculpture itself is a decorative Mickey, not a Hidden Mickey.)

Hither, Thither & Yon Scavenger Hunt

The Water Parks, Downtown Disney & Beyond

A car is the most efficient method for hunting the following areas. I've planned the hunt taking time of day and location into consideration. However, some backtracking will help keep you ahead of the crowds. Don't forget to be courteous to the shoppers, diners, golfers, swimmers, other guests, and cast members you encounter during your hunt.

Because you may want to hunt only one area at a time, I've listed the perfect score for each area in parentheses after its name in the Clues section.

The Golf Courses
(9 points)

If you're a golfer, look for the following Hidden Mickeys:

Clue 1: A classic Mickey sand trap on the Magnolia Golf Course.
4 points

Clue 2: A putting green shaped like Mickey Mouse at the Bonnet Creek Golf Club (home of the Eagle Pines and Osprey Ridge courses). You can visit this Hidden Mickey without playing golf.
5 points

Walt Disney World Speedway
(5 points)

Clue 3: Go to the racetrack to take a look at the lake on the infield, or more accurately, a photo of it. You have to be in the grandstands to

135

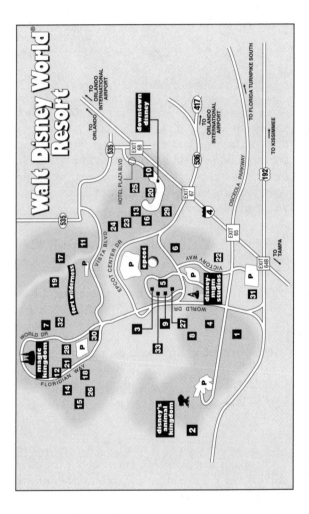

1	All-Star Resorts	19	Pioneer Hall
2	Animal Kingdom Lodge	20	Pleasure Island, in Downtown Disney
3	Beach Club	21	Polynesian
4	Blizzard Beach	22	Pop Century
5	BoardWalk	23	Port Orleans French Quarter
6	Caribbean Beach	24	Port Orleans Riverside
7	Contemporary	25	Saratoga Springs
8	Coronado Springs	26	Shades of Green
9	Dolphin	27	Swan
10	Downtown Disney	28	Transportation and Ticket Center
11	Eagle Pines Golf Course	29	Typhoon Lagoon
12	Grand Floridian	30	WDW Speedway
13	Lake Buena Vista Golf Course	31	Wide World of Sports
14	Magnolia Golf Course	32	Wilderness Lodge
15	Oak Trails Golf Course	33	Yacht Club
16	Old Key West	P	Parking
17	Osprey Ridge Golf Course		
18	Palm Golf Course		

137

get an overview of the lake (it's barely visible from the fence around the parking area for the *Richard Petty Driving Experience*), and grandstands are only put up for races. So check out a framed photo of the racetrack inside the guest sign-in building to find this classic Mickey. If you want to see it with your own eyes, you will have to go to the races and ante up for admission.
5 points

Water Parks
(19 points)

★ *Blizzard Beach* (19 points)

Clue 4: On the wall at the right rear of the Beach Haus store, near the dressing rooms, take a close look at the light cover.
3 points

Clue 5: In the Lottawatta Lodge counter service restaurant, find a classic Mickey on the chimney.
3 points

Clue 6: Look for a "Hidden Lizard" in the rocks behind Melt-Away Bay.
4 points

Clue 7: Spot a classic Mickey formed by three round rocks on the ground near one of the support poles for the *Chairlift* ride. Psst! You can see it to the right of the *Chairlift* gondola.
4 points

(Tip: The singles line for the *Chairlift* is usually shorter than the regular line, but you can bypass the *Chairlift* if you want. "Climb" the mountain, via the stairs, to the Observation Deck to spot this Mickey.)

Clue 8: Go to the rear of the park (by tube or on foot) to find a classic Mickey with a sorcerer's hat that's formed by three jutting stones topped by a small triangular rock. Psst! He's near the center of the side of a stone bridge that crosses over Cross Country Creek.
5 points

★ *Typhoon Lagoon* (0 points)

The Mickster may be hiding in here, but I have yet to find a convincing Hidden Mickey on the premises of Typhoon Lagoon!

Disney's Wide World of Sports
(5 points)

Clue 9: Search hard for a three-dimensional Mickey Mouse head near the high central ceiling of The Milk House (the Field House). He's on an upper rafter opposite the main entrance. Hard to find but worth it!
5 points

Downtown Disney West Side
(41 points)

★ *Cirque du Soleil* (3 points)

Clue 10: Head for the outside restrooms (they're under the main entrance staircase to the theater) and examine the tiles on the floor in either one (men's or women's). See a small classic Mickey?
3 points for either

★ *DisneyQuest* (28 points)

Clue 11: Toward the end of the pre-show video, during the entrance elevator ride, find a classic Mickey formed by three small spheres.
3 points

Clue 12: Check out the carpets on the third and fifth floors (in, respectively, Ventureport and The FoodQuest dining area).
3 points for both

Clue 13: Look for track lighting shaped like a classic Mickey on the second through fifth floors. Psst! It's not on the same side on all four floors.
5 points for all four

Clue 14: Find similar lighting near "Invasion! An ExtraTERRORestrial Alien Encounter."
3 points

Clue 15: Spot classic Mickey markings on the back of one of the creatures you encounter during "Aladdin's Magic Carpet Ride." (You don't have to take the ride; you can watch the overhead video screens as others ride.)
3 points

★ Find two classic Hidden Mickeys at the "Virtual Jungle Cruise." (Again, you needn't take the ride; you can stand behind one of the ride pods and watch.)

Clue 16: Before the ride starts, watch the left side of the screen.
4 points

Clue 17: Keep watching the screen during the first part of the ride to see if the raft exits a glacier area. (The riders have optional routes, so they may not enter the glacier area.) If it does, watch carefully as it exits. (The ears on this Hidden Mickey aren't perfectly formed, but you'll recognize them.)
3 points

Clue 18: Along the queue for "Pirates of the Caribbean," examine the walls for Hidden Mickeys.
2 points

Clue 19: Check out the trash can and the floor at the exit.
2 points for both

★ *Wolfgang Puck Café* (5 points)

Clue 20: Study the mosaic tile pyramid behind the receptionist counter to find a classic Hidden Mickey.
5 points

★ *Disney's Candy Cauldron* (4 points)

Clue 21: Go inside to find a classic Mickey marking on a stone.
4 points

★ *Mickey's Groove* (1 point)

Clue 22: Observe the logo.
1 point

Downtown Disney Marketplace
(73 points)

★ *Entrance to the Marketplace* (4 points)

Clue 23: Check out the signs over the entrances.
1 point for one or more

Clue 24: Examine the interactive flat fountain at the entrance near the bus depot. Find any classic Mickeys?
3 points for two types

★ *Goofy's Candy Co.* (4 points)

Clue 25: Spot Hidden Mickeys in the candy paintings inside.
2 points

Clue 26: Look around for Mickey-shaped candies.
2 points

★ *Disney's Days of Christmas* (6 points)

Clue 27: Step inside and find at least one classic Mickey on each of three large trees.
4 points total for one or more on each tree

Clue 28: Take a good look at the ceiling in the rear room of the shop.
2 points

★ *Once Upon A Toy* (17 points)

(This store sports numerous Mickeys and other Disney characters in the décor in addition to the Hidden Mickeys below.)

Clue 29: Find several classic Mickeys in the cement outside.
2 points

Clue 30: Examine the snowflakes in a window display. Psst! Look for two types of Hidden Mickeys.
3 points for both

Clue 31: Outside the main entrance, look for classic Mickeys with tires for ears.
1 point

★ Now enter the store and keep your eyes open.

Clue 32: Check out the tops of merchandise stands. Psst! Only some sport Hidden Mickeys.
1 point

Clue 33: Now examine the bottom of these stands.
1 point

Clue 34: Look at the upper beams of the wooden merchandise displays.
1 point

Clue 35: Now observe the bolts on those displays.
1 point

Clue 36: Observe the pincers (holding toys) in the room with Mr. PoTato Head.
1 point

Clue 37: Examine the mural behind the service desk in the same room.
1 point

Clue 38: Find a classic Mickey cloud in a central room.
3 points

Clue 39: Look for Hidden Mickey lollipops.
2 points

★ *Team Mickey Athletic Club* (5 points)

Clue 40: Find a Hidden Mickey in the Disney Vacation Club (DVC) display near Team Mickey.
2 points

Clue 41: Inside the store, check the tops of the mannequin heads and merchandise stands.
3 points for two types

★ **Near the Lake** (5 points)

Clue 42: Spot classic Mickeys in the fence around the lake.
1 point

Clue 43: Search the "World's Largest Perikaleidoscope" for classic Mickeys.
4 points for two types

★ **World of Disney** (32 points)

Clue 44: Find light brown classic Mickeys outside the store.
2 points

Clue 45: Look for classic Mickeys in some of the clothing racks.
2 points

Clue 46: In the high-ceilinged central room, find an upside-down classic Mickey on the Pocahontas airship.
4 points

★ Now find two classic Mickeys on the Tweedle Dee and Tweedle Dum mural in the same room.

Clue 47: Look for a flag.
2 points

Clue 48: Check out an apron.
2 points

Clue 49: Find a classic Mickey emblem on the Chinese Theater in another wall mural in the same room.
4 points

Clue 50: Spot classic Mickeys on paintings in the central Genie Room.
2 points

Clue 51: In this room, look carefully for Hidden Mickeys in the wallpaper.
3 points

Clue 52: In the same room, observe the "antique" maps decorating the walls. Psst! Think character profiles.
5 points for three

Clue 53: Next door in the Villain Room, spot Cruella DeVille's Hidden Mickey.
3 points

Clue 54: In the Alice in Wonderland Room, take a close look at a playing card in one of the wall murals.
3 points

Miniature Golf Courses
(12 points)

You can find Hidden Mickeys while you play the courses. Or you may be able to walk the courses without playing if it's not crowded, due to rain or luck. (Tell the attendants that you're hunting Hidden Mickeys and ask if you can take a look around.)

★ *Fantasia Gardens* (4 points)

Clue 55: Check the tee-off areas.
1 point

Clue 56: Take a good look at the 12th hole on the Gardens Course.
3 points

★ *Winter Summerland* (8 points)

Head straight for the 16th holes to find the Hidden Mickeys on these courses.

Clue 57: Spot Goofy and Donald on the 16th hole of the Snow Course.
3 points

Clue 58: Now check around the same hole for a Mickey Mouse gingerbread cookie.
2 points

Clue 59: Find Mickey and Minnie Mouse on the 16th hole of the Sun Course. Psst! This Hidden Mickey is also visible from the 16th and 17th holes of the Snow Course.
3 points

Pleasure Island
(16 points)

★ *D-Zertz shop* (5 points)

Clue 60: Spot Mickey Mouse behind the D-Zertz shop.
5 points

★ *Comedy Warehouse* (11 points)

There are usually five shows nightly, starting at about 7:30 p.m. (or later).

Clue 61: Try to spot a classic Mickey inside, on a wall to the left.
4 points

Clue 62: Spot the classic Mickey sign to the left of the stage.
3 points

Clue 63: Now look to the right of the stage to find another classic Mickey on the wall.
4 points

Near Celebration, Florida
(4 points)

Okay, I admit it; this Mickey isn't hidden. Just the opposite, in fact. But it is unique. So I decided to include it anyway. You'll find a huge classic Mickey near Celebration, Florida, on the west side of Interstate 4.

Clue 64: Look for it as you get close to Exit 62.
4 points

Total Points for Hither, Thither & Yon =

How'd you do?

A perfect score for this scavenger hunt is 184. But here is a breakdown by area, so that you can tally your score for only those areas you've covered. You'll find the perfect score for each section in parentheses. Give yourself gold if you score at least 80% of available points.

The Golf Courses (9)

Walt Disney World Speedway (5)

The Water Parks (19)
   Blizzard Beach (19)
   Typhoon Lagoon (0)

Disney's Wide World of Sports (5)

Downtown Disney West Side (41)
   Cirque du Soleil (3)
   DisneyQuest (28)
   Wolfgang Puck Café (5)
   Disney's Candy Cauldron (4)
   Mickey's Groove (1)

Downtown Disney Marketplace (73)
   Entrance to the Marketplace (4)
   Goofy's Candy Co. (4)
   Disney's Days of Christmas (6)
   Once Upon A Toy (17)
   Team Mickey Athletic Club (5)
   Near the Lake (5)
   World of Disney (32)

Miniature Golf Courses (12)
   Fantasia Gardens (4)
   Winter Summerland (8)

Pleasure Island (16)
   Behind the D-Zertz shop (5)
   Comedy Warehouse (11)
   Near Celebration, Florida (4)

**Caution:
Don't peek at this
section unless you
really want help!**

The Golf Courses

Hint 1: A sand trap at the sixth green of the Magnolia Golf Course is shaped like a classic Mickey.

Hint 2: The putting green at the Bonnet Creek Golf Club (Eagle Pines and Osprey Ridge Golf Courses) is shaped like a side profile of Mickey Mouse.

Walt Disney World Speedway

Hint 3: A lake on the infield is shaped like a classic Mickey. You can see it "live" from the grandstand if you go to the track to watch an Indy race, and it's often visible on your home TV screen during televised races. Visit the Speedway at other times and you'll barely see the lake, let alone the Hidden Mickey. To marvel at its full effect without paying an admission, walk inside the guest sign-in building and look at the framed photo on the wall.

Water Parks

- Blizzard Beach

Hint 4: Find a lighting fixture on the wall at the right rear of the Beach Haus store near the dressing rooms. There's a painting on the cover in which a small classic Mickey is formed by rocks at the lower center of an outdoor mountain scene.

Hint 5: Above the fireplace near the food order area in the Lottawatta Lodge counter service restaurant, a classic Mickey is formed by three stones in the center of the chimney, about halfway between the mantelpiece and the ceiling.

Hint 6: At the top of the rocky hill at the rear of Melt-Away Bay, just right of center, the highest rock forms a lizard's snout. His left front foot is visible on the rock below.

Hint 7: Near the *Chairlift* ride that takes you to the water slides, on the second level of the mountain, look to the ground just past support pole #4 to spot a classic Mickey made of three round rocks. This Hidden Mickey is visible from two places, near the top of the *Chairlift* ride (to the front and right of the gondola) and from the left corner of the Observation Deck (where it is visible under the *Chairlift*). If you ride the *Chairlift* to see it, enjoy a water slide or a walk back down the mountain.

Hint 8: At the rear of the park, a classic Mickey is formed by three stones jutting out from near the top edge of a stone bridge crossing Cross Country Creek. It is on the side of the bridge, near the center. A small triangular rock over this Hidden Mickey gives it the appearance of wearing a sorcerer's hat.

You can see this Mickey from the water or dry land. It's visible from the floating tubes as you approach the bridge and, on land, you can see it through the trees either from in front of the "Runoff Rapids" entrance sign or from several points on the walkway on the other side of the bridge.

Disney's Wide World of Sports

Hint 9: A three-dimensional Mickey Mouse head looks out over the court from near the high central ceiling in The Milk House (the Field House). He's on an upper rafter above "The Milk House" sign, in front of a yellow triangular wall partition that is opposite the main entrance. I spotted him to the upper left of the lower seats of section 104.

Downtown Disney West Side

- *Cirque du Soleil*

Hint 10: Under the main entrance staircase to the Cirque du Soleil show are restrooms for men and women. You'll find tiles laid to approximate a small classic Hidden Mickey on the floors of both restrooms, in a corner just inside the entrance doors. The circles don't touch, but the design is convincing enough for me.

- *DisneyQuest*

Hint 11: Toward the end of the pre-show video, during the entrance elevator ride, a classic Mickey is formed by three spheres at the bottom of a ray gun. (This Hidden Mickey is more convincing than the spheres at the bottom of the large three-dimensional ray gun poised over the lobby of Ventureport.)

Hint 12: Symbols and figures that include classic Mickey designs are woven into the carpets on the third and fifth floors in, respectively, Ventureport and The FoodQuest dining area.

Hint 13: Track lighting shaped like a classic Mickey hangs above the elevator doors on floors two, three, four, and five. You'll find it near the "Mighty Ducks Pinball Slam" (on the third floor) and near "Ride the Comix" (on the fourth and fifth floors). On the second floor, near "CyberSpace Mountain," the lighting is above an elevator door on the opposite side of the elevator bank.

Hint 14: Similar track lighting can be found in front of pod 4 of "Invasion! An ExtraTERRORestrial Alien Encounter."

Hint 15: During "Aladdin's Magic Carpet Ride," the golden beetle you encounter bears classic Mickey markings on its back.

Hint 16: At the "Virtual Jungle Cruise," classic Mickey-shaped balloons periodically float up from the left side of the screen, in front of the castle, before the ride starts.

Hint 17: On the screen in the first part of the "Virtual Jungle Cruise" ride, the raft may exit a glacier area under a distorted classic Mickey-shaped ice bridge over the river.

Hint 18: In the wall murals along the queue for "Pirates of the Caribbean," the rightmost set of palm tree coconuts near the stairs is shaped like a classic Mickey.

Hint 19: The DisneyQuest classic Mickey logo is on trash cans (like the one near the exit) and is illuminated on the floor of the exit walkway.

- Wolfgang Puck Café

Hint 20: Behind the receptionist counter, about two thirds the way up the mosaic pyramid, a white tile and two smaller black tiles form a classic Mickey. Search for it to the right of a tall ceramic vessel standing on a shelf.

- Disney's Candy Cauldron

Hint 21: Inside the store, on the upper wall above the candy display, a dark marking on a stone near the ceiling forms a classic Hidden Mickey.

- Mickey's Groove

Hint 22: Above the entrance doors, a classic Mickey forms the middle of the Mickey's Groove logo.

Downtown Disney Marketplace

- Entrance to the Marketplace

Hint 23: Signs over the entrances to the Marketplace sport classic Mickeys at their sides.

Hint 24: At the Marketplace entrance near the bus depot, each water tube head in the interactive flat fountain is shaped like a classic Mickey, and the waterspouts are arranged to form a classic Mickey on the surface.

- Goofy's Candy Co.

Hint 25: Classic Mickey candies adorn the pictures over the door to the Earl of Sandwich eatery.

Hint: 26: Juicy classic Mickey candies are in the lighted rightmost photo on the rear wall and also in lower photos to the left of the leftmost candy display.

- Disney's Days of Christmas

Hint 27: Inside the shop, three large trees surrounded by merchandise have classic Mickeys carved in their bark near the tops of their trunks. The trees are not Christmas trees, and each of the three has one or two Mickey carvings.

Hint 28: In the rear room of the shop, classic Mickeys are in the scrollwork on the ceiling.

- Once Upon A Toy

Hint 29: Outside the store, you'll find several classic Mickeys in the cement near the side entrance.

Hint 30: In a window display near the side entrance, snowflakes contain both classic and full length Hidden Mickeys along with other Hidden characters.

Hint 31: Outside the main entrance, classic Mickeys are formed by truck tires (the ears)

151

on top of Lincoln Log columns.

Hint 32: Tinker Toys on top of merchandise stands around the store form classic Mickeys.

Hint 33: At the bottom of these merchandise stands, you'll find classic Mickey supports.

Hint 34: The center of the upper beams on wooden merchandise displays sport classic Mickey shapes.

Hint 35: Also on the wooden merchandise displays, large wing nuts on some of the bolts form Mickey ears.

Hint 36: Classic Mickey pincers (holding toys) circulate on a track hanging from the ceiling in the room with Mr. PoTato Head.

Hint 37: In this same room, the mural behind a service desk includes a classic Mickey balloon.

Hint 38: In a central room of the store, a classic Mickey cloud appears in a window of a mural behind the service desk.

Hint 39: In the rear room, lollipops are arranged to form classic Mickeys on the outside of the castle and merchandise stands.

- Team Mickey Athletic Club

Hint 40: Outside the entrance to Team Mickey, a classic Mickey is repeated in the white picket fence bordering the Disney Vacation Club display.

Hint 41: Some of the mannequin heads and merchandise stands inside the store are topped with classic Mickeys, with a basketball for the head and a baseball and a tennis ball for the ears.

- Near the Lake

Hint 42: Several sections of the green fence around the lake have repeating classic Mickeys near the top of the railing.

Hint 43: On the Marketplace walkway near the World of Disney store, the "World's Largest Peri-kaleidoscope" has classic Mickeys behind glass in the viewing areas and outside along the walls of the tower.

- World of Disney

Hint 44: Light brown classic Mickeys can be found near the top of the columns outside the store.

Hint 45: Classic Mickey holes are drilled in some of the metal posts that hold up clothing racks.

Hint 46: In the high-ceilinged central room, the Pocahontas airship has an upside-down classic Mickey at the very bottom of the rear vertical tail fin, near where the tail fin connects to the body of the airship.

Hint 47: In the same room, you'll find a classic Mickey on a flag in the background of the Tweedle Dee and Tweedle Dum wall mural.

Hint 48: That mural also includes a classic Mickey on Tweedle Dee's apron.

Hint 49: In the same room, behind the three little pigs floating overhead, another wall mural has a classic Mickey emblem above the doors of the Chinese Theater.

Hint 50: On the walls in the central Genie Room, classic Mickeys can be spotted near the tops of the compass paintings.

Hint 51: Subtle classic Mickeys hide in the red wallpaper in the display cabinets. They're visible if you change your angle of view.

Hint 52: Also on the Genie Room walls, antique-looking maps on wood panels painted to look like tapestries have land masses that resemble the side profiles of Mickey Mouse, Goofy, Winnie the Pooh, and possibly Donald Duck. (Donald is a bit of a stretch.)

Hint 53: On the wall in the Villain Room, next door to the Genie Room, Cruella DeVille's left wrist is wrapped with fur that has a classic Mickey dark spot on the side.

Hint 54: In the Alice in Wonderland Room at the side of the store, a wall mural includes a three of Clubs playing card with an upside-down, black classic Mickey marking.

Miniature Golf Courses

- *Fantasia Gardens*

Hint 55: The tee-off areas here are marked with classic Mickeys.

Hint 56: On the Gardens Course, the green at the 12th hole is shaped like a classic Mickey.

- *Winter Summerland*

Hint 57: On the 16th hole of the Snow Course, you'll find Goofy and Donald nutcrackers on the left side of the mantelpiece.

Hint 58: A Mickey Mouse gingerbread cookie pokes out from a stocking hanging on the right side of the same mantelpiece.

Hint 59: On the left side of the 16th hole of the Sun Course, Mickey and Minnie Mouse are sitting in a sleigh on the mantelpiece. Since the 16th holes of both courses are close together, this Hidden Mickey is also visible from the 16th and 17th holes of the Snow Course.

Pleasure Island

- D-Zertz shop

Hint 60: A large Mickey Mouse is peeking over the wall at the rear of the alcove behind the D-Zertz shop. His fingers and part of his head are visible.

- Comedy Warehouse

Hint 61: Inside on a wall to the left, near the sound and light control booth, a round Walt Disney World Band logo (on a square sign) is the head of a classic Mickey. The ears are a round Walt Disney World Railroad sign and an octagonal speed limit sign. It's not a perfect classic Mickey, but it's close enough for me.

Hint 62: On the rear wall to the left (as you face the stage), you'll see a classic Mickey sign that reads, "KOCO – Oklahoma City."

Hint 63: On the wall to the right of the stage, a spoked wheel with a clock in the center is the head of a classic Mickey and two drums form his ears. One is a Mickey Mouse Club drum and the other a drum with red and white spirals.

Near Celebration, Florida

Hint 64: On the west side of Interstate 4, south of exit 62 near Celebration, Florida, you'll find a huge classic Mickey atop an electrical transmission line pole.

Other Mickey Appearances

• •

These Hidden Mickeys won't earn you any points, but you're bound to enjoy them if you're in the right place at the right time to see them.

★ Look for holiday Hidden Mickeys if you're at Walt Disney World during the Christmas season. For example, the "Osborne Family Spectacle of Lights" along the backlot area at Disney-MGM Studios includes many hiding Mickeys.

★ Other "Hidden" Mickeys — décor and deliberate — appear with some regularity throughout WDW. Notice the Mickster on WDW brochures, maps and flags, cast member name tags, guest room keys, pay telephones and phone books, and restaurant and store receipts. The restaurants offer classic Mickey butter and margarine pats, pancakes and waffles, pizzas and pasta, as well as Mickey napkins. They also arrange dishes and condiments to form classic Mickeys, and some condiment containers are shaped like Mickey.

The Mickey hat and ears on top of the Earffel Tower are obvious to every visitor in the vicinity of Disney-MGM Studios. Many road signs on WDW Resort property sport Mickey ears, and WDW vehicles and monorails have Mickey Mouse insignia.

Cleaning personnel will often spray the ground, windows, furniture, and other items with three circles of cleaning solution (a classic Mickey) before the final cleansing. Or they may leave three wet Mickey Mouse circles on the pavement after mopping! Mickey even decorates manhole covers, survey markers, and utility covers in the ground, as you've had a chance to find out for yourself on some of the scavenger hunts.

Enjoy all these Hidden Mickeys as you enjoy WDW. And if you want to take some home with you, rest assured that you can always find Hidden Mickeys on souvenir mugs, merchandise bags and boxes, T-shirts, and Christmas tree ornaments sold in the Disney World shops. So even when you're far away from WDW, you can continue to enjoy Hidden Mickeys.

CHAPTE

HIDDEN MIC

by door
fun to

My Fa
Hidden

In this book, I've described almost 500 Hidden Mickeys at Walt Disney World. I enjoy every one of them, but the following are extra special to me. They're special because of their uniqueness, their deep camouflage (which makes them especially hard to find), or the "Eureka!" response they elicit when I spot them — or any combination of the above. Here then are my Top Ten Hidden Mickeys and, not far behind, Ten Honorable Mentions. I apologize to you if your favorite Hidden Mickey is not (yet) on the lists below.

My Top Ten

1. Mickey in the mural above the entrance to *Body Wars*, Wonders of Life Pavilion, Epcot. This Mickey Mouse wins the trophy as the grandest Hidden Mickey at Walt Disney World Resort. The Best of the Best!

2. Mickey hiding behind the fern on the big mural inside the Garden Grill Restaurant, The Land Pavilion, Epcot. When I outline this Mickey (a cast member often hands me a broom to reach it), I have witnessed folks in the restaurant smile and shout "I see him; look, there's Mickey!"

3. Mickey peeking over the fence behind the D-Zertz shop, Pleasure Island, Downtown Disney. Awesome!

4. Minnie Mouse's shadow on the mural by the loading dock, *The Great Movie Ride*, Disney-MGM Studios. Once you see her, you'll never forget her.

5. Mickey sitting with Donald on the wall, "Raiders of the Lost Ark" scene, *The Great Movie Ride*, Disney-MGM Studios. A real regal Mickey.

6. Mickey in the vines outside the rear lob-

, Animal Kingdom Lodge Resort. Hard to find, spot.

. Mickey sitting on the edge of the roof of a building next to the Contemporary Resort. A playful Mickey who welcomes you to the Magic Kingdom.

8. The "Grim Reaper" Mickey, *The Haunted Mansion*, Liberty Square, Magic Kingdom. A classic.

9. The big Mickey outlined in the cement at the rear of Africa, Disney's Animal Kingdom. Hard to find. One of the largest and most inventive classic Mickeys.

10. Mickey with his sorcerer's at on the side of a bridge over Cross Country Creek in Blizzard Beach water park. Exhilarating!

Ten Honorable Mentions

1. Mickey in the rafters in The Milk House (the Field House), Disney's Wide World of Sports. The Main Mouse benevolently watches over his minions.

2. Profiles of Mickey and other characters in the Genie Room, the World of Disney store, Downtown Disney Marketplace. Quality art work.

3. Impressions in the cement sidewalk on Sunset Boulevard with the name "Mortimer" (the name originally proposed for Mickey), Disney-MGM Studios. Show off your knowledge of Disney lore.

4. Mickey's profile in the moon, wall mural at Toy Story Pizza Planet Arcade, Disney-MGM Studios. One of the best Mickey profiles anywhere.

5. Mickey's image in the moss on *The Tree of Life*, Disney's Animal Kingdom. A majestic classic Mickey, hiding in plain sight.

6. The utility cover classic Mickey by the Tamu Tamu Refreshment Shop, Africa, Disney's Animal Kingdom. The mundane utility cover transformed.

7. Mickey in the rock by the fireplace, Wilderness Lodge Resort lobby. One to be proud of, an awesome Hidden Mickey.

8. The tiny Mickey on the counter of the Kona Island Coffee Bar, Polynesian Resort. Simple but irresistible.

9. The shell Mickeys in the sidewalk, Old Key West Resort. A satisfying discovery, worth the effort!

10. Last but not least, the huge Hidden Jafar along the Pangani Forest Exploration Trail in Disney's Animal Kingdom. The sight will take your breath away.

• •

Hidden Mickey mania is contagious. The benign pastime of searching out Hidden Mickeys has escalated into a bona fide vacation mission for many Walt Disney World fans. I'm happy to add my name to the list of converts. Searching for images of the Main Mouse can enhance a solo trip to the parks or a vacation for the entire family. Little ones delight in spotting and greeting Mickey Mouse characters in the parks and restaurants. As children grow, the Hidden Mickey game is a natural evolution of their fondness for the Mouse.

Join the search! With alert eyes and mind, you can spot Hidden Mickey classics and new ones waiting to be found. Even beginners have happened upon a new, unreported Hidden Mickey or two. As new attractions open and older ones get refurbished, new Hidden Mickeys await discovery.

It may be just my imagination but I swear that every time I visit Walt Disney World, I spot a Hidden Mickey up in the clouds, watching over his domain! Do you think the Imagineers might actually have some influence on the atmosphere over Walt Disney World?

The Disney entertainment phenomenon is unique in many ways, and Hidden Mickey mania is one manifestation of Disney's universal appeal. Join in the fun! Maybe I'll see you at Disney World, marveling (like me) at the Hidden Gems. They're waiting patiently for you to discover them.

CHAPTER 11

Index to Mickey's Hiding Places

Note: This Index includes only those rides, restaurants, hotels, and other places and attractions that harbor confirmed Hidden Mickeys. So if the attraction you're looking for isn't included, Mickey isn't hiding there. Or if he is, I haven't yet spotted him.

– Steve Barrett

The following abbreviations appear in this Index:

AK - Disney's Animal Kingdom
DD - Downtown Disney
DM - Disney-MGM Studios
E   - Epcot
MK - Magic Kingdom
WP - Water Parks

A

B

C

D